JANE ELLEN HARRISON

Anthropology's Ancestors

Edited by Aleksandar Bošković, Institute of Archaeology, Belgrade.

As anthropology developed across geographical, historical and social boundaries, it was always influenced by works of exceptional scholars who pushed research topics in new and original directions and who can be regarded as important ancestors of the discipline. The aim of this series is to offer introductions to these major figures, whose works constitute landmarks and are essential reading for students of anthropology, but who are also of interest for scholars in the humanities and social sciences more generally. In doing so, it offers important insights into some of the basic questions facing humanity.

Volume 10
Jane Ellen Harrison
Robert M. Stroup

Volume 9
Zora Neale Hurston
Ana Gretel Echazú Böschemeier and Peti Mama Gomes

Volume 8
Ibn Khaldun
Lawrence Rosen

Volume 7
Elsdon Best
Jeffrey Paparoa Holman & Frederico Delgado Rosa

Volume 6
Max Gluckman
Hugh Macmillan

Volume 5
Alfred Cort Haddon: A Very English Savage
Ciarán Walsh

Volume 4
Mary Douglas
Paul Richards and Perri 6

Volume 3
Françoise Héritier
Gérald Gaillard

Volume 2
William Robertson Smith
Aleksandar Bošković

Volume 1
Margaret Mead
Paul Shankman

For a full volume listing, please see the series page on our website: http://berghahnbooks.com/series/anthropologys-ancestors

JANE ELLEN
HARRISON

Robert M. Stroup

berghahn
NEW YORK • OXFORD
www.berghahnbooks.com

First published in 2026 by
Berghahn Books
www.berghahnbooks.com

Library of Congress Cataloging-in-Publication Data

A C.I.P. cataloging record is available from the Library of Congress
Library of Congress Cataloging in Publication Control Number: 2026946933

British Library Cataloguing in Publication Data

A catalogue record for this book is available from the British Library

EU GPSR Authorized Representative

LOGOS EUROPE, 9 rue Nicolas Poussin, 17000, LA ROCHELLE, France
Email: Contact@logoseurope.eu

ISBN 978-1-80758-051-3 hardback
ISBN 978-1-80758-054-4 paperback
ISBN 978-1-80758-050-6 epub
ISBN 978-1-80758-052-0 web pdf

https://doi.org/10.3167/9781807580513

CONTENTS

ILLUSTRATIONS

FOREWORD

Aleksandar Bošković

A FORGOTTEN ANCESTRESS

This book introduces an ancestor—more precisely, an ancestress—that many people in contemporary anthropology had not heard of. And yet, the importance of work by Jane Ellen Harrison, her influence and her ideas, have profoundly shaped scholarship —primarily in the classics—throughout the last century. The foremost twentieth-century scholar of Classical Greek religion, Walter Burkert (1931–2015) was heavily influenced by her. This is obvious in his works, even when he does not quote her directly. Furthermore, as put by one of the world's leading Classical scholars, Mary Beard, in her book about Harrison:

> Jane Ellen Harrison changed the way we think about the ancient Greeks; she infuriated the academic establishment at the turn of the nineteenth and twentieth centuries with her uncompromising refusal to play the submissive part; she fell repeatedly and hopelessly in love - usually with entirely unsuitable men, who were also her academic colleagues; she gave some of the most remarkably theatrical lectures that the University of Cambridge has ever seen; in the very male intellectual world of a century ago, she put women academics and women's colleges (dangerously) on the map. (Beard 2000: xi)

As a matter of fact, "Jane Ellen Harrison changed the way we think about ancient Greek culture - peeling back that calm, white marble exterior to reveal something much more violent, messy and ecstatic underneath" (Beard 2010). This is, of course, similar

to Frazer's view of his own (British) contemporary culture, so, as he was embarking on his work on Pausanias (second century BC *Description of Greece*), Frazer wrote in 1884 to his publisher George Macmillan that his work (the edition of Pausanias' books) would clearly show "the underlying savagery within the Graeco-Roman and Christian tradition" (qtd. in Stocking 1995: 138–39).

Jane Ellen Harrison was also, in her own way, what we would call today an "engaged anthropologist," she lectured publicly and promoted science, including most recent archeological discoveries, bringing cultures distant in both time and space to contemporary audiences, with great skill:

> Flamboyantly dressed and armed with what were hailed as the most up-to-the-minute visual aids, in the form of stunning lantern slides, she drew vast crowds to her open lectures – on one occasion, so she said, attracting 1600 fans in Glasgow to a presentation on the topic of Athenian tomb sculpture. She even created something of the same atmosphere in her university lectures. "The hushed audience would catch the nervous tension of her bearing," wrote one of her academic colleagues about her teaching of classical archaeology. "Every lecture was a drama." (Beard 2024)

Harrison's influence on anthropology is today rarely mentioned, even though she referred to herself as an "anthropologist"—for example, in the polemical article, written probably around 1912, "Homo sum" (this is also how this text is signed, Harrison, n.d.: 31). In this short text, she eloquently promoted the idea that women should have the right to vote, using various examples from anthropology. Like many other works, this one seems also ahead of her time—despite being very well written and politically, highly relevant.

Jane Ellen Harrison came to be regarded as the best representative of the "Myth and Ritual School" (or "Cambridge Ritualists," as they were sometimes known), even with some ambivalence of this "school's" attitude to J. G. Frazer (Ackerman 1991, 2007). While Frazer is regarded as a key influence on this

group of scholars, Ackerman, as well as Segal (1980) convincingly argue that Harrison was the most important representative of this group of scholars (Bošković 2021: 92–93), and her acceptance of some of the major theories of her time (Freud's and Durkheim's) made her an important interlocutor in wider contemporary theoretical debates on myth and religion. In one of her most famous books, *Themis*, Harrison wrote, "The primary meaning of myth in religion is just the same as in early literature; it is the spoken correlative of the sacred rite, the thing done; it is to legomenon [old Greek: 'something said only once'—A. B.] as contrasted with, or rather as related to, to dromenon [old Greek: 'things done'—A. B.]." (1912: 328). This is an important practical aspect of the interpretation of human behavior—a critical step that brings one from description to understanding.

This is also a very anthropological attitude. Anthropologists have always been busy trying to understand different cultures, and Harrison was also trying to use the comparative method: "I have been investigating lately the origins of religion among primitive peoples, and this has led me to observe the customs of South Sea islanders and North American Indians." (n.d.: 4) She also used other disciplines, like art, archeology, social psychology, and sociology, all of which contributed to the richness of her work and the depth of her insights. French philosopher Bergson's 1907 book *L'Évolution Créatrice* was an important influence, and A. R. (Radcliffe) Brown's 1909 lectures in Cambridge introduced her to Durkheim's theories (Lloyd-Jones 2007). Of course, as noted by one of her contemporary interpreters, Beard (2010, 2024), her arguments (especially the two major studies that she published in 1903 and 1912) are not always easy to follow, and she was much more popular among the more educated readers.

For (mostly) academic audiences, Harrison was re-discovered in the late 1960s and early 1970s following the work of Burkert, especially *Homo Necans* (1972), as well as in the studies of several French Classical historians (like Jean-Pierre Vernant [1914–2007]).

Burkert claimed that Harrison introduced functionalism (through her emphasis on the role of community and the rituals

performed by members of the society) in the studies of antiquity—as well as in anthropology. Ackerman's works point to the important relationship of her work to Frazer's. Of course, Frazer never really liked her work (nor any other of the "Ritualist school"), even though Harrison considered him as her teacher (Segal 1999: 41).

Through this complicated web of relationships, and her dialogue with different authors, a more complex image of Jane Ellen Harrison emerges. It is worth pointing out that, despite what comes out as her celebrity status, at the time when she was associated with Cambridge (1898–1922), "Women's colleges weren't formally part of the university; women students could take university exams but, in the worst of both worlds, they did not actually receive a degree if they passed; and a woman, such as Harrison, who lectured on university property did so strictly by invitation only." (Beard 2024). Unfortunately, social sciences (and anthropology is no exception) have traditionally sidelined or conveniently "forgotten" female scholars—and this is the topic that could probably merit at least another volume. One of the efforts that the series in which this book is published (Anthropology's Ancestors) is to correct this imbalance and set the record straight.

Harrison was, of course, a woman of her time, and subsequent scholarship has proven many of her ideas and theories wrong. Evolutionism already became unfashionable during her lifetime, and authors like Bachofen faded into obscurity. However, no single scholar in recent history had so thoroughly changed our perspective on a civilization that remains an important part of contemporary intellectual heritage. This had an immediate effect on anthropology, not just through one of its founding fathers (Frazer—with all his skepticism), but also Murray, who was Harrison's lifelong friend and supporter, and who was influential in Oxford's anthropological circles. At the same time, very few scholars had influenced so many different disciplines as Harrison did, while at the same time serving as important role models. I hope that the present volume will make readers curious about her research and inspire them to take their own journeys of discovery, like Harrison did in her youth.

REFERENCES

Ackerman, Robert. 1991. *The Myth and Ritual School: J. G. Frazer and the Cambridge Ritualists.* New York: Garland Publishing.

———. 2007. "Cambridge Ritualists [Ritual Anthropologists]." *Oxford Dictionary of National Biography.* Retrieved June 19, 2018 from https://doi.org/10.1093/ref:odnb/95519.

Beard, Mary. 2000. *The Invention of Jane Harrison.* (Revealing Antiquity, 14). Cambridge (MA): Harvard University Press.

———. 2010. "My Hero: Jane Ellen Harrison." *The Guardian* September 4. Retrieved July 24, 2024 from https://www.theguardian.com/books/2010/sep/04/mary-ellen-harrison-mary-beard.

———. 2024. "Iron in the Soul." *London Review of Books* Vol. 46 No. 17, September 12. Retrieved December 30, 2024 from https://www.lrb.co.uk/the-paper/v46/n17/mary-beard/iron-in-the-soul.

Bošković, Aleksandar. 2021. *William Robertson Smith.* (Anthropology's Ancestors, 2). New York: Berghahn Books.

Burkert, Walter. [1972] 1983. *Homo Necans: The Anthropology of Ancient Greek Sacrificial Ritual and Myth.* Berkeley and Los Angeles: University of California Press.

Harrison, Jane Ellen. 1912. *Themis: A Study of the Social Origin of Greek Religion.* Cambridge: Cambridge University Press.

———. n.d. "'Homo sum' being a Letter to an Anti-Suffragist from an Anthropologist." 2nd edition. Westminster: The National Union of Women's Suffrage Societies.

Lloyd-Jones, Hugh. 2007. "Harrison, Jane Ellen (1850–1928)." *Oxford Dictionary of National Biography.* Retrieved April 9, 2020 from https://doi.org/10.1093/ref:odnb/33734.

Segal, Robert. 1980. "In Defense of Mythology: The History of Modern Theories of Myth." *Annals of Scholarship* 1: 3–49.

———. 1999. *Theorizing about Myth.* Amherst: University of Massachusetts Press.

Stocking, George W. 1995. *After Tylor: British Social Anthropology, 1888–1951.* Madison: University of Wisconsin Press.

INTRODUCTION

Just over a century ago Jane Ellen Harrison radically transformed the study of Greek religion. Until then, classics had been dominated by textual analysis and philology, but by incorporating findings from the then-new scholarly disciplines of archeology and ancient art, psychology, anthropology and sociology, the theories of evolution advanced by Darwin, and the ideas about primordial matriarchal religion advanced by Bachofen she forced a re-evaluation of our understanding of Greek religion. Today it is difficult to imagine the study of classics limited to literary studies, important as they are, without the amplifying findings of archeology, art, anthropology, sociology, and so many other perspectives. Yet in her time, the relevance of art and archeology was strenuously resisted by many established classicists. Harrison transformed the study of Greek religion by making it interdisciplinary and by presenting radically new ways of seeing Greek religion, particularly by attending to its often obscure and brutal rituals. For many years, Harrison's ideas exercised a strong influence on the classicists and students of Greek religion who followed her.

Mary Beard has described Harrison as "the first woman in England to become an academic, in the fully professional sense – an ambitious, full-time, salaried, university researcher and lecturer" (2010). While Harrison remains a feminist icon and role model, and the subject of many recent biographical studies, her works have recently almost disappeared from the reading lists in classics departments and from the awareness of the general reading public. I find this dismaying and a great injustice. To my mind,

her work remains important in part because her hypotheses provided the groundwork for later generations of students of Greek religion—but also because in her writings, she constructed a new vision of Greek religion, new understandings of its goddesses and gods, and its rituals and myths that remains radical. Her work was that of a brave intellectual explorer who, in the face of heavy academic resistance, forged new and larger ways of investigation in classics. Her books still deserve to be read.

In this volume, we will explore Harrison's radically new vision of Greek religion. We will see how Harrison the "ritualist" revised the dominant view of the role of ritual in Greek religion and ritual's relation to myth, and how her own views shifted over time. We will examine the ways she transformed the study of classics by incorporating the methods and ideas derived from archeology, art, psychology, anthropology and sociology, and the science of evolution. Finally, I will show how Harrison's deeply felt sense of the presence of the numinous in Greek religion, especially in the mystery cults of late antiquity, contributed not only to a renewed appreciation of the experiential aspect of Greek religion for its practitioners in antiquity, but also to a revival of a recognition of the existential pertinence of Greek religion in various forms to our own deepest experiences (as articulated by Walter Otto,[1] Karl Kerényi,[2] and James Hillman,[3] among others).

Harrison is remembered today, somewhat erroneously, as the founding member of the so-called "Cambridge Ritualists." The term "ritualist" is somewhat misleading because she did not originate the idea of ritualism, a concept usually attributed to William Robertson Smith[4] and James George Frazer,[5] nor were her attitudes toward the relationship between myth and ritual consistent. While Harrison always considered myth to be related to ritual in some essential manner, how she visualized this relation was somewhat inconsistent even in her early work. She came to summarize this relation in her famous aphorism: "myth is ritual misunderstood." By this, like William Robertson Smith, she meant that myths were invented to explain rituals, (hence the term "etiological myths"). She emphasized that the rituals still practiced in the classical period were often incalculably old and

their purposes and functions had frequently been forgotten, but their continued observance was due to religion's innate conservatism. She pointed to the detailed artistic descriptions of rituals (such as on vase paintings) to show that a given ritual and its associated myth often did not align. She concluded that the myth was newer and had been invented to provide an explanation for an otherwise now inexplicable ritual. Harrison surrounded herself with a circle of younger, like-minded men who came later to be referred to as the "Cambridge Ritualists" (a name they never used themselves). This group, including Gilbert Murray, Francis Cornford, and A.B. Cook, saw ritual as arising with and associated with myth, and opposed themselves to the old (and still widely accepted) view that ritual is merely myth enacted.

Today the argument over the primacy of ritual versus myth has largely passed. A rough consensus has evolved that the question of primacy of one or the other may not be answerable and may vary from case to case. Students of myth and ritual have come to agree that, by and large, the two go together. Before Harrison, classicists had generally focused on myth, particularly in its readily available literary renditions. I suspect that Harrison's early attention to rituals grew out of her innate love of Greek art. Very early on in her work, she discerned discrepancies between the descriptions of rituals as they appeared in texts and in how they were portrayed in art. These discrepancies opened up a radically new approach to understanding Greek religion. She discovered strata of Greek religion that seemed to have been glossed over by later literary tradition. By identifying ways in which later texts differed from and "betrayed" older traditions depicted in painting and sculpture, Harrison may be said to have anticipated the post-modern "hermeneutics of suspicion" of the later twentieth century.

Harrison's innovative perspective had at least three sources: the intellectual world of her time and place, the particularities of her biographical background and education (which will be discussed in the next chapter), and her unique genius.

Harrison's identification of the mostly submerged stratum of Greek religion, dominated by chthonic, dark, often ill-defined deities, transformed the study of Greek religion in her own time

and is now widely accepted. Later scholarship has had to take this chthonic stratum into any substantive account of the history of Greek religion. In his *Homo Necans* (1972), Walter Burkert, perhaps the most highly regarded contemporary interpreter of Greek religion, locates a violent, murderous strain running through early human culture and purports to find evidence for this in the initial stages of Greek religion. His hypothesis is a clear reflection of Harrison's idea about the chthonic; *Homo Necans* would be impossible without the groundwork laid by Harrison.[6]

The intellectual climate of the late nineteenth century—what we might call Harrison's world—was dominated by a number of "great ideas." These include advances in the new fields of anthropology, comparative religions, and linguistics prompted by engagement with hitherto unknown peoples in the wake of the European colonial project. They also include Darwin's theory of evolution, which made such an enormous impact on the thinking in all fields of study. To these we may add the "Woman Question" and Johann Jakob Bachofen's suggestion that a Primordial Goddess religion preceded the patriarchal religion of the archaic and classical periods, and the philosophy of Nietzsche with its valorization of the irrational. Finally, the decline of organized religion in Europe and new discoveries about so-called "primitive" religions gave rise to questions regarding the origins and evolution of religions, the function of religions, the relation of ritual and mythology, and the future of religions.

By the "Woman Question," I mean the generalized sense of unease about established views of gender raised by the rapid appearance in Europe's bigger cities of large numbers of single, unattached women who lived alone or with other women, worked outside the home, made their own money and their own decisions independently from men. Harrison was one such independent woman and her identification as such by herself and others colored her intellectual endeavors and their reception.

Johann Jakob Bachofen brought together questions about the taken-for-granted inferiority of the feminine and religious evolution in his theories about a Primordial Goddess religion. His ideas re-appear in Harrison's work in her theories about the

historical primacy of the great Goddess and in the ongoing centrality of goddesses in women's cults in later periods and in many of the mystery cults.[7] As later on Harrison became aware of the work of Freud, she found this perspective corroborated by the prominence Freud gives to the mother in the psychic life of us all, as is reflected in the Oedipus complex. In the beginning, both psychologically and historically, she is there.

Harrison, like many others of her time, not only accepted Bachofen's ideas but greatly expanded upon them. Matriarchy and goddess religion appealed to Harrison at a deep level, perhaps reflecting her upbringing, perhaps as a reaction to her own experience of the deep-seated sexism of her time, likely both. Harrison brought needed attention to the primacy, centrality, and potency of the goddesses. She insisted that goddesses had been present from the very beginning of Greek religiosity, although initially they were nameless, formless, inchoate.

The philosophical ideas of Nietzsche were "in the air" of the late nineteenth century and Harrison seems to have found them irresistible.[8] She was especially drawn to his recognition of the importance of the unconscious and of repression and the "return of the repressed."[9] Nietzsche's ideas may have helped her to expand on Bachofen's idea of the repression and occlusion of the earlier goddess religion, and to understand how elements from this earlier goddess religion would later reappear in the emergence of the mystery cults.

In Harrison's earliest studies of Greek religion, which she initially approached through the study of art before later incorporating the then-new discoveries arriving from anthropology and archeology, she found herself unexpectedly and profoundly moved by certain, specific aspects of Greek religion: the goddesses, the submerged, chthonic aspects of early Greek religion, and the mysticism of the much later mystery cults. That is, without ever stating so explicitly, Harrison describes the experienced reality of these aspects of Greek religion for the Greeks in a way that suggests that she found herself drawn into an experiencing of the reality of the numinous which she had never found in Christianity.

Harrison's description of the *keres*, the chthonic deities and their rites (especially the women's secret rites), the partially obscured and submerged goddesses, and the mystery rites strongly suggests a direct, felt familiarity with these aspects of Greek religion that is not explained by mere intellectual understanding. Harrison's descriptions of the awe and dread attendant upon rites such as the Anthesteria, the Thesmophoria, and the nocturnal sacrifices to the chthonic deities betray, if unintentionally, her own profoundly experienced awe and dread in the presence of the inchoate realities present in and underlying these rites.

Until well into the nineteenth century, Greek religion was often idealized as representing the perfection of beauty, rationality, and balance. Today, thanks in large measure to Harrison's innovative proposals, students of Greek religion recognize that the religion of ancient Greece, like all religions past and present, had its dark, chthonic, terrifying aspects.

Harrison described early Greek religion as very different from the worship of the Olympian gods described in Homer and so often idealized in later centuries. She revealed the existence of a dark, chthonic stratum of Greek religion, devoted to Underworld goddesses and gods especially, and worshipped in night-time rituals of purgation and placation. She brought to light a pantheon of spiritual entities representing various modes of the embodiment of death and disease (the *keres*). These precursors to the anthropomorphic gods of the Greeks might be entirely disembodied and aniconic, partially embodied, theriomorphic, or anthropomorphic.

> Our minds are imbued with current classical mythology, our imagination peopled with the vivid personalities, the clear-cut outlines of the Olympian gods; it is only by a somewhat severe mental effort that we realize the fact essential to our study that *there were no gods at all* ... (Harrison 1991: 163–64)

In the nineteenth century archeology was not respected by contemporary classicists.[10] Harrison faced great opposition at

Cambridge University to her incorporation of the findings of archeologists in her work. At that time classics was dominated by philology, with its heavy emphasis on texts and text-based hermeneutics. Thus, for Harrison to bring non-textual findings from art and archeology into her work in the field was seen as a radical innovation. She was, by nature, a visually oriented person. It took great courage to follow her gift for visual aesthetics, not only in re-evaluating long-familiar works of art but also in emphasizing the immense value of the artifacts newly unearthed by archeologists. In doing so, she vastly expanded our understanding of Greek religion. Yet in 1903 when Harrison published *Prolegomena to the Study of Greek Religion*, it was well-received at Cambridge University and immediately became a textbook (Ackerman 1991b: xiii).

Harrison's incorporation of the perspectives of cultural anthropology was both a brilliant innovation and a principal reason for the erosion of her standing as a scholar. The then-dominant tenet of evolutionary anthropology, holding that all cultures originate in similar circumstances and evolve through similar stages, allowed her to suggest an outline of how Greek religion might have evolved as parallel to developments elsewhere. When the theory of a universal pattern of cultural evolution came under severe criticism in the mid-twentieth century, the positive view of Harrison's theories declined with them.

Prolegomena was written at a time when Harrison was going through a serious personal upheaval and suffering from depression, which may have driven her toward a reckoning with her own unconscious and laid the groundwork for her encounter with the numinous. Her later writings (especially *Themis* [1912]) are more cogently written but they lack the urgency of an actually felt, overwhelming experience.

Harrison's *Prolegomena* was subjective, idiosyncratic, and highly controversial at the time of its publication and remains so today. The ongoing controversy arises from her speculations about the nature of early Greek religion, some of which have not been corroborated by later research. It helps to begin by recognizing that our knowledge of Greek culture in general and of

Greek religion in particular is inescapably deficient and likely to remain so. Consciously or not, scholars fill in the lacunae of our knowledge with what they suspect or believe to be fact, but which is to a large degree conjecture. Even as more ancient manuscripts and other artifacts come to light and serve to add incrementally to our partial understanding of Greek religion, its rituals and myths, our knowledge will always remain to a large degree incomplete. We can never truly understand the Greek mind of the archaic and classical periods because we cannot know what given symbols, rituals, words, gods, and myths meant to the original worshippers.

Harrison discovered an earlier Greek religion based on the placation of malignant, Underworld *daemones*, ancestor spirits, *keres*, and chthonic deities that remained active beneath and behind the more familiar gods of Olympian religion. She uncovered a stratum of dark, chthonic, and daemonic Greek religion, myth, ritual, and art that was "hidden in plain sight." This stratum was much older and deeper than the later, Olympian layer celebrated by poets of the archaic age, such as Homer, Hesiod, and the author(s) of the Homeric Hymns.

> ... festivals which are nominally connected with, or as the handbooks say, 'celebrated in honor of' various Olympians; the Diasia in honour of Zeus, the Thargelia of Apollo and Artemis, the Anthesteria of Dionysos. The service of these Olympians we should expect to be of the nature of joyous 'tendance.' To our surprise, when the actual rites are examined, we shall find that they have little or nothing to do with the particular Olympian to whom they are supposed to be addressed; that they are not in the main rites of burnt-sacrifice, of joy and feasting and agonistic contests, but rites of a gloomy underworld character, connected mainly with purification and the worship of ghosts. The conclusion is almost forced upon us that we have here a theological stratification, that the rites of the Olympians have been superimposed on another order of worship. The contrast between the two classes of rites is so marked, so sharp, that

> the unbroken development from one to the other is felt to be almost impossible. (Harrison 1991: 10–11)

She believed that after the occlusion of the goddess religion by the arrival of the Aryans' male sky-gods, the goddesses and their cults persisted in the form of a cultural "unconscious," an underlying religious stratum of women's cults, partially out of view, that later—as the hold of the male-god dominated Olympian religion weakened in later antiquity—re-emerged in the mystery cults.[11]

Harrison's account of the *keres* is hair-raising. She makes us feel them as still alive, regardless of the names we apply to them or to how we imagine them physically or artistically. Who has not felt the almost physically real, almost embodied presence of disease, fear, or death?

Harrison's account of the Greek goddesses, in marked contrast to her account of the gods, clearly reveals her love for the submerged mother goddesses and her keenly-felt sense of their reality and power—a love we can see re-emerging in recent years in the goddess worship of many second-wave feminists, neopagans, and Wiccans. Some have suggested that this hunger for the mother goddess, for the divine female, was channeled by the Church into Marian devotion, where at times, it threatened to eclipse Mary's divine Son in popular devotion. Harrison can be seen as tapping into a universal longing for reconnection to the source of our being.

Many Jungian and post-Jungian scholars, perhaps pre-eminently James Hillman, have testified to their experience of the gods and goddesses of the Olympian pantheon as psychological realities who act mythically in and through our lives. But Harrison, (and also Karl Kerényi, to his great credit), do not limit themselves to the divinities of the classical period, but acknowledge the never-dimmed potency of all aspects of Greek religion: rituals, mysteries, processions, symbols, verbal formulae, and superstitions.

Moving into the second half of *Prolegomena* feels like entering a different world. Following her exploration of the power of the chthonic, the *keres*, the goddesses, and their associated rituals in

early Greek religion, Harrison turned her attention to the much later cult of Dionysos and Orphism. The text devoted to these two subjects grew in size to double the length of an already lengthy volume. This turn occurred because in 1900, while she was writing *Prolegomena*, she met Gilbert Murray, who was working on *Bacchae*, Euripides' play on Dionysos and his followers, and its connection to Dionysian rites. Harrison wrote to Murray:

> It's rather dreadful, the whole centre of gravity of the book has shifted. It began as a treatise on Keres with a supplementary notice on Dionysus. It is ending as a screed on Dionysus with an introductory talk about Keres. Whose fault is that? *Never, never* again will I ask you to lecture when I am writing a book, a nice sound one too, it was, till last autumn. (qtd. in Ackerman 1991b: xxvi–xxvii)

Not only was Harrison enthusiastic about collaborating on a project of mutual interest with her friend and colleague, but more importantly, she was discovering the still-vital power of a religion thought to be long-dead. Just as in her study of the chthonic elements of early Greek religion and the pre-Olympian goddesses she had begun to experience for herself their numinous power, so now in her study of Dionysos and the Mystery religions she experienced their still-living power. Harrison's writing leaves us with a strong sense that for her Dionysos, too, exerted the pull of "of gravity" and that she felt his numinous power.

In this way, Harrison made yet another radical discovery about how religions are born. At a time when the dominant intellectual climate viewed religion as a primitive relic of the past, a superstition destined to be overcome by logic, science, and positivism, Harrison saw that new religions may arise by the re-emergence of an older religion. The Eleusinian cult preceded worship of the Olympian gods but gained its greatest prominence after the polis-centered Olympian religion began to wane. The Greeks of the classical period viewed Dionysos as an "outsider" and he was never fully accepted as an Olympian god, but in the Orphism of later antiquity he was the most important deity.

Harrison's discovery that not only do religions die, but that they are also born and re-born, has ongoing relevance. When a religion begins to die, the hunger for profound experience of the numinous and transcendence persists and may find expression not only in the creation of a new religion or by taking on the religion of another culture, but in the revitalization of elements from ancient, long-neglected traditions. Harrison's account of the cult of Dionysos anticipates the modern-day search for ecstasy and altered states of consciousness through psychedelic drugs and other non-traditional spiritual practices.

Thus, the second half of *Prolegomena* is devoted to exploring the ways in which a religion can re-invent itself after a lengthy period of decline and exhaustion; by reviving, recycling, and reinterpreting older deities, symbols, myths, and rituals, to arrive at an apparently new religion that addresses unaddressed spiritual and cultural needs.

Curiously, in *Prolegomena* Harrison discusses one of the most important elements in all of Greek religion, the Eleusinian Mysteries; not as part of her early discussion of the two goddesses, but in a chapter called "Orphic and Dionysiac Mysteries." She makes the very original and rather startling claim that: "all in [the Eleusinian Mysteries] that was not a primitive harvest festival, all or nearly all their spiritual significance, was due to elements borrowed from the cult of Dionysos" (Harrison 1991: 539). This is startling because the Mysteries had long been thought to be centered entirely on the two goddesses Demeter and Persephone and their myths. Citing both literary and artistic evidence, she claims that Dionysos was not a late addition to the Eleusinian Mysteries but rather, an essential figure from its beginning. She believes that at Eleusis, Dionysos was the divine consort of the Mother goddess as well as her divine son, Brimos. Harrison identifies the ecstatic experiences that occurred in the Eleusinian Mysteries as Dionysian in origin. She saw the death-conquering aspects of the Mysteries as arising not only from the ancient vegetation and fertility cult of Demeter and Persephone, but also from the cult of Dionysos, the dying and reappearing god.

In Harrison's *Themis* (1912), published nine years after *Prolegomena* (1903), she radically revised her theories about the origins about the goddesses and the gods by taking into account the sociological theories of Durkheim, Bergson's philosophical ideas, and Freud's psychology. It is arguably her ideas about the social origin of ritual put forward in *Themis* for which Harrison is best remembered. Yet, despite the greater clarity and organization in how her ideas are expressed in *Themis* and the greater enthusiasm with which this book was received, her earlier, less well-organized *Prolegomena* remains, at least in my eyes, more intriguing. In *Prolegomena*, Harrison was still struggling with her ideas and was not yet entirely certain of what she thought. This uncertainty, perhaps inadvertently, led to an infusion of her own psychological struggles to a greater degree than in her later works.

To help us understand this personal aspect of Harrison's enthusiasm for early Greek religion it may be helpful to turn to the thought of her near contemporary, Sigmund Freud. Harrison was born in 1850, five and a half years before Freud. His *Interpretation of Dreams*, published in November 1899, sold only 351 copies in six years. Freud's public fame came not from *Interpretation of Dreams*, but rather in 1901 with the publication of *The Psychopathology of Everyday Life*. Harrison claims to have been greatly affected by his works and to have incorporated his ideas into her later works, most especially in *Themis*. *Prolegomena to the Study of Greek Religion* was written before Freud was widely known. Although at the time Harrison was writing *Prolegomena* she was unaware of Freud's work, parallels between the perspectives of these near contemporaries are intriguing. Many of the intellectual currents prevalent in the late nineteenth century so visible in Harrison's works are addressed as well in those of Freud and other early depth psychologists. These include ideas about the origins and evolution of religion, the roles of taboo and ambivalence, the revalorization of the "feminine" and the lifelong importance of the Mother, the powerful effects of repression, resistance, and projection. But the most important common theme is that

of the excavation of the "chthonic." Freud often spoke of his discovery of the unconscious as an entry into the Underworld of Greek mythology, into the chthonic realm that so fascinated Harrison, the buried, the unearthed, the partially forgotten, occluded Underworld.

Her excavation of the Underworld of Greek religion coincided with the beginnings of depth psychology, with Freud's discovery of the unconscious, which he so often visualized as an Underworld. The historical tendency to divert attention from the submerged, chthonic level of Greek religion is uncannily similar to how our psyches do their utmost to avoid the contents of the unconscious. Both realms, mythological and psychological, are perceived as underground, feared, unseen. Freud taught us that when the unconscious is allowed to speak, it will yield an unexpected wealth of healing. Likewise, Harrison showed that the partially submerged world of chthonic deities, rituals, mysteries, and myths re-emerged in the Greek world during the sixth and fifth centuries in response to needs that were insufficiently addressed by the dominant Olympian religion; creating a late flourishing in Greek religion with the rise of Orphism and the mystery cults—forms that led by various paths into early Christianity. Given that Harrison and Freud did not know of one another at the time *Prolegomena* was written (Freud seems never to have known of Harrison's work), the parallels in their writing, the emphases on the unearthing of the chthonic, are as unmistakable as they are unexpected.

There are also important connections between Harrison's work and that of C. G. Jung. Both recognized that religion was more than "things done," "things shown," and "things said." Harrison's attraction to the study of Greek religion may have reflected an unacknowledged desire to understand what lay at the root of her own spiritual inclinations, something she had ignored after rejecting the religion of her upbringing. Jung, and less explicitly Harrison, invite us to explore the possibility that at a deep but unacknowledged level we mourn the loss of a necessary connection with the spiritual or religious aspects of life and that we seek an experiential connection to the sacred.[12]

Harrison's experience of certain aspects of Greek religion is an instance of what Rudolph Otto describes in *The Idea of the Holy* (1917): it is experiential, not belief, not dogma.[13] Harrison detected the smoldering embers of numinosity in a locus long thought to be dead. She showed us a pathway through the deeply buried ruins in the underworld of our Western culture, showed us the life still present there beneath the ashes, and she provided us, Ariadne-like, with the blood-red thread of inner life to follow from antiquity to the present; the thread of spirit, ritual, myth, symbol, and mystery.

By pursuing her passion for visual aesthetics, Harrison the skeptical academic surprised herself by discovering a living core of genuine spiritual experience lying at the heart of Greek religion, whose Olympian aspects she had considered to be effete, exhausted of religious passion, and largely functional. Harrison may have felt the need to suppress her own, unrecognized spiritual nature by her early exposure to the exaggerated emotional expressions of evangelical Christianity of her childhood—a religion whose emotional excesses were a source of embarrassment to her in later life. It may be that her passion for visual aesthetic experience, her love for the visual arts and for Greek religion, provided a way for her to experience spiritual life on her own terms. Orphism may have appealed to her more reserved, restrained personality in ways that evangelical Christianity could not. Alternatively, the goddesses and the mystery religions may have appealed to precisely those aspects of her personality that she had suppressed early in life out of necessity: her love for the missing mother, her ardently loving nature that was thwarted repeatedly, a passionate nature that might have reveled on the mountainsides with the raving Maenads had she been born in ancient Greece rather than Victorian England.

Harrison appears to have stumbled across elements of genuine spiritual life in the pursuit of what I believe to have been, at the conscious level, purely academic study. In the process of examining the religion of another people she began to sense the presence of something missing in her culture and in her own life. It has long been noted that our Western culture has become very

one-sided, favoring the material, the rational, the scientific and neglecting the world of the spiritual, the unconscious, the emotional and non-rational. Yet a culture's greatest treasure is its experience of the sacred. However, since this experience is ineffable, it is transmitted in the guise of religion, encrusted with rituals, practices, symbols, myth, and allegory. Many of the rituals have lost their original meanings and functions, and many of the symbols and myths are obscure, yielding up their significance only after extended contemplation and the expenditure of great effort. These difficulties evoke a certain degree of skepticism. Religious skepticism is not unique to the modern era. The Greeks, too, were skeptical of their polis-centered, Zeus-dominated religion as is shown by some of the tragedians, particularly Euripides, by the Sophists, and even by Plato and Aristotle, and, of course by the Orphics and the adherents of the mystery cults.

Harrison rejected Christianity very early in life, as did so many other intellectuals of the late nineteenth century. The internal one-sidedness created by this rejection of her childhood religion and the empirical, scientific, materialistic attitude of the academy with its neglect of the spiritual and emotional, the spontaneous and unconscious, may have led to a process of *enantiodromia*, [the psychological process first described by C. G. Jung, in which an excessive emphasis on one aspect of the conscious life elicits the emergence of its opposite in the unconscious]. By eliciting such *enantiodromia* she was able to rediscover in her work those spiritual aspects she had earlier left behind. She seems to have stumbled across true spiritual and emotional connection with aspects of Greek religion: goddesses, the chthonic, and especially the mysteries and Orphism.

Harrison and Freud, pioneers in their respective fields, proceeded necessarily by intuition and feeling, guesswork and imagination. They occasionally stumbled but they were not abashed by their mistakes. Instead of fearing to address their errors, they eagerly revised their theories, always acknowledging that theirs were works in progress. Neither was afraid of employing their subjective experience as a hermeneutic. Freud famously did so by analyzing

himself after his father's death and so coming to terms with his own Oedipus complex. Harrison was more discreet in acknowledging the biographical and emotional sources of her insights and intuitions, never openly recognizing them. However, aspects from her personal and emotional life are reflected in the idiosyncratic nature of the insights that resulted from her investigations into Greek religion: in her focus on the submerged, the erased, the invisible, and nearly invisible yet still powerful Feminine. Indeed, the "submerged, erased, yet powerful Feminine" could, in fact, serve as a metaphor for a brilliant, academically ambitious woman of Harrison's time—that is for Harrison herself.

Harrison was motivated by what moved her deeply, by what she loved, by her aesthetic appreciation of the exquisite beauty of Greek art. Consciously, she was relying on her gift for rational thought to pursue what was at bottom a non-rational, sensual love of the beautiful. Harrison's writings about goddesses, the chthonic, and especially, the mysteries betray a surprising degree of feeling: it offended her that the ancient goddesses had been supplanted and submerged. In her account of the occlusion and replacement of the goddesses and the chthonic deities we can feel that she is describing herself—ignored, belittled, and sidelined by the sexist, male-dominated academic establishment that had little or no interest in her thoughts. Harrison was the supplanted goddess. She was the occluded chthonic religion.

Harrison's experience of exclusion and devaluation allowed, even forced her, to see a similar process as having occurred in the history of Greek religion.

A woman of her brilliance and ability, struggling against the strong gender prejudice of her time (of which she complained very little), was necessarily faced with the obvious fact of the repression or radical devaluation of all things feminine. While she built to an extent on Bachofen's theories, Harrison's own theory that the early primacy of goddess-religion in Greece was supplanted and suppressed by a later patriarchal religion, sounds remarkably like her experience of being a woman in Victorian England. That is, she was aware of the power and value of women and their relationships with one another, beginning

with herself, her love for her mother whom she lost so early, the love she had for her women friends and for her female colleagues—and aware that all of this was so often dismissed. In her own life and her work, she demonstrated feminine power and how it resisted its overshadowing, repression, and dismissal by masculine culture.

It is perhaps still insufficiently recognized that our intellectual endeavors reflect, to at least some degree, our social milieu: family and upbringing, social class, ethnicity, and gender. Much of the criticism of Harrison's work has to do with her incorporation of ideas that were current during her lifetime but are now disparaged. However, even if we no longer accept the nineteenth-century image of a universal pattern of cultural evolution (with its positing of "primitive" origins and an inevitable progression from "lower" to "higher"), can we not recognize the significant changes that occurred over time in Greek religion? Even if we have come to doubt the evidence supporting the theory that in Europe worship of goddesses wholly predated worship of gods, can we not recognize the ways in which goddess cults and women's cults were, indeed, cast in the shadow of the cults of male gods, suppressed, and denigrated?

The attitude of skepticism toward religion, a process of disenchantment that began in the Renaissance, gained strength in the Enlightenment, and crested in the nineteenth and twentieth centuries, continues today to dominate in academic and intellectual circles. Harrison began her work with this mental framework of religious skepticism, but she was later captivated by certain elements of Greek religion, especially the mystery cults and women's cults, feeling their real, living power. Although the process of "re-enchantment" of religion began before Harrison with German Romantics such as Friedrich von Schlegel and the poet Friedrich Hölderlin, she was one of the most prominent scholars of Greek religion to bring sustained attention to this process and to introduce it into the greater academic world. This re-enchantment of Greek religion was continued after her by scholars such as Walter Otto, Karl Kerényi, James Hillman, and Christine Downing.[14]

Harrison, like Freud and the other early depth psychologists, was a pioneer in her field and very aware of the unknown terrain she faced. The fact that she revised her theories later in life and was open to criticism of them demonstrates that she knew she was speculating rather than stating hard fact. Yet despite her early errors, too often trumpeted by later critics, she opened up new territory for investigation. If the timeline of Harrison's theory of the evolution of Greek religion has come under criticism, we must nonetheless recognize that individual elements of her work still hold up: the goddesses may not have preceded the gods, but the goddesses and many other elements of earlier Greek religion were indeed driven underground.

In the chapters that follow, we will explore the ways in which Harrison employed a variety of "outside" disciplines in her transformation of the study of Greek religion: art and archeology, sociology and anthropology, ritualism, and mystical religion.

NOTES

1. Walter Friedrich Gustav Hermann Otto (1874–1958), classicist and student of Greek religion, is today best known for his works *The Homeric Gods* (1929) and *Dionysos* (1933), in which he argues for the reality of the Greek gods as forces of Nature and as the sources of religious experience for the Greeks. Artistic representations in sculpture and, above all, in epic poetry and tragedy, tended to humanize the gods and to empty them of divinity, bringing them "down to earth." Since literature and art are nearly all of what have come down to us, many modern readers of Greek literature came to believe that the Greeks of the classical era no longer truly "believed" in their gods as divine powers, accepting that the Greeks saw their gods as they were depicted in the Homeric epics: as effete figures, dramatic actors only, that had lost all or most of any religious authenticity they had ever possessed. Walter Otto was one of the earliest to recognize the religious, spiritual reality that the gods continued to possess for the Greeks despite their depiction in epics and drama.
2. Karl Kerényi (1897–1943), also a classical philologist and student of Greek religion, was greatly influenced by Walter Otto. In collaboration with Carl Gustav Jung (1875–1961) he developed a psychologically influenced study of mythology. This collaboration resulted in the two essays *Das göttliche Kind in mythologischer und psychologischer Beleuchtung*

(*The Myths of the Divine Child*) and *Das göttliche Mädchen* (*The Divine Maiden*), published together as *Einführung in das Wesen der Mythologie* (*Essays on a Science of Mythology*) (1941).

3. James Hillman's (1926–2011) psychological system, termed archetypal psychology, builds upon Jungian analytical psychology. Hillman's work relies heavily on Walter Otto and on their shared understanding of polytheism. In Hillman's view, the gods and their associated myths both reflect the workings of the human mind and provide an ordering function to our lives. He stresses the importance of identifying myths that we are living through and the gods that are "living through us."
4. William Robertson Smith (1846–1894) is considered, with James George Frazer, the originator of the "myth and ritual school," emphasizing the priority of ritual over myth. His book *Lectures on the Religion of the Semites* (1889) was published in same year as Frazer's *The Golden Bough.* Both had a profound influence on Jane Harrison's thought, especially in *Prolegomena.* For Robertson Smith, primitive religion was primarily a matter of "things done," not things believed, rituals rather than dogma. Consequently, he asserted that myth was derived from ritual, not ritual from myth, as most students of religion at that time, being text-based, believed. Harrison's earlier thinking, as reflected in *Prolegomena*, was essentially the same as Smith's: "myth is ritual misunderstood." In her later writings, *Themis* and *Ancient Art and Ritual,* Harrison altered her views and moved beyond this somewhat rigid formulation.
5. James George Frazer (1854–1941), folklorist and social anthropologist, was a close friend of William Robertson Smith and was greatly influenced by him. He was one of the earliest writers in the myth and ritual school. His best-known book, *The Golden Bough*, was first published in two volumes in 1890, with later editions in 1900 (three volumes) and 1915 (twelve volumes), and an abridged single volume edition published in 1922. This book became widely known and read and had an enormous influence, not only in anthropology. T. S. Eliot cites *The Golden Bough* in the footnotes to his poem "The Wasteland"; Sigmund Freud cites his work in *Totem and Taboo* (1950). Jane Harrison was greatly influenced as well by his work and that of Robertson Smith, as will be discussed in Chapter 3, "Harrison's Ritual Theories."
6. Walter Burkert (1931–2015), arguably the most prominent author of Greek religion of the late twentieth century, in his *Homo Necans* (1983) acknowledges his reliance on Harrison's work, especially her *Themis.* Burkert recognizes the importance of ritual in Greek religion and the many ways in which ritual and myth are related without addressing the controversy over the priority of the one over the other. Burkert's book *Greek Religion* (1985) not only describes the religion of the Greeks as it

existed in the classical era but also explores the origins of the gods and the history of the rituals. Burkert's writings incorporate a century of archeological and academic progress made since Harrison's time, yet his writing is reminiscent of Harrison's, having the feel of excavation of the hidden and buried prehistory Greek religion. Like Harrison, he forces the realization of how unfamiliar to us the Greek gods truly are, and how strange and foreign are their rituals.

7. Johann Jakob Bachofen (1815–1857) is today best known for his 1861 book *Das Mutterrecht* (*Mother Right*), in which he postulated a prehistoric stage of social, political and religious matriarchy. This highly speculative theory had great influence upon subsequent generations of thought. Not only Jane Harrison, but also Marija Gimbutas (*The Goddesses and Gods of Old Europe* [1974], among many others) and Robert Graves (*The Greek Myths* [1955] and *The White Goddess* [1948]) expanded upon Bachofen's theory of the primordial matriarchy. Joseph Campbell assumes primordial matriarchy as factual and bases much of his writing on this. Psychologists relying on this theory include C.G. Jung, Erich Fromm, and Erich Neumann (author of *The Great Mother* [2015]). Friedrich Engels based his work *The Origin of the Family, Private Property and the State* (1884) on the ideas of Bachofen. Often neglected is the fact that Bachofen saw matriarchy (Mother Right) as only the second of four phases in the evolution of the social order toward its ultimate achievement of patriarchy, which he viewed as the sum and goal of this evolution. (The matriarchal phase was preceded by a primitive "Hetaeric" phase of communal sexual attachments and followed by, first the partially patriarchal "Dionysian" phase and finally by the fully patriarchal "Apollonian" phase, in which true civilization would emerge.)

   While later investigation has failed to support the theory of primordial matriarchy, it retains importance because it brought needed attention to feminine aspects of antiquity including goddesses and their cults, the cults of women, harvest and fertility, and to all aspects of the lives of women in antiquity.

8. As a classicist Friedrich Wilhelm Nietzsche (1844–1900) is perhaps best known today for the iconoclastic *The Birth of Tragedy Out of the Spirit of Music*, (1872). Nietzsche's fascination with Dionysos (but not as much with Apollo) appears in Harrison's *Prolegomena*, in which Harrison devotes nearly half of the book to Dionysos and Dionysian and Orphic religion. Nietzsche's influence on Harrison's *Prolegomena* is more broadly pervasive, however, as is evident in her skeptical attitude toward the "sunny" Olympian religion in general, her excavation of dark, powerful, feminine forces that had been (with only partial success) repressed by later patriarchal forces and that this showed through as a "bad conscience" in the culture and religion of classical Greece.

9. Many of the ideas and terms associated with Freud and psychoanalysis originated with Nietzsche—a fact that Freud acknowledged although he claimed that he long avoided reading Nietzsche in order not to be influenced by him. "Repression" (*Hemmung*) is only one such term that Freud took up from Nietzsche. A complete listing of such influences and terms is too great to give at length but we may list among these the idea of the unconscious, the Id ("It" in English, Nietzsche and Freud having employed the German "Es" [It]), the "unmasking" trend of psychoanalysis, the dynamic concept of the mind with its aggressive and self-destructive drives, defense mechanisms, sublimation, father and mother imago, resentment, false consciousness, false morality, and the "illness" of civilization (Ellenberger 1970: 277).
10. This is all the more surprising in view of the astounding archeological discoveries made around this time by Heinrich Schliemann at Troy and Mycenae and by Sir Arthur Evans in Crete.
11. Harrison's formulation of a religious and cultural "return of the repressed," written at almost the same time as Freud's *Interpretation of Dreams* (1899), uncannily mirrors Freud's formulation of this process occurring on a psychological basis. Freud's work was, as yet, unknown at the time.
12. Carl Gustav Jung was the son of a Protestant minister and had been expected to follow his father in the ministry but, like Harrison, he rejected the traditional Christianity of his upbringing. However, his writings betray a mystical tendency, which many have interpreted as a persistent, deep yearning for the numinous, a replacement for the lost religion of his childhood.
13. Rudolph Otto (1869–1937), theologian and student of religion, opposed the skeptical, demystifying Enlightenment attitude toward religion that had gathered force through the nineteenth century. In *The Idea of the Holy* (1917), he introduces the term "the numinous" as part of an attempt to describe phenomenologically the experiential aspects of religion, further characterizing the mystical experience of religion as "*mysterium tremendum et fascinans.*" Harrison abandoned the Christianity of her childhood and never returned to it, assuming the skeptical attitude toward religion characteristic of her time. However, as will be discussed in Chapter 4, she seems to have been caught up, possibly to her great surprise, by the power of the goddesses of prehistoric Greece and to have experienced something of the "*mysterium tremendum and fascinans*" of these awesome, often nameless goddesses.
14. Christine Downing (b. 1931) in her book *The Goddess* (1981) explores the many ways in which the Greek goddesses of the Olympian pantheon live on in the life and self-understanding of a contemporary woman.

CHAPTER 1

HARRISON'S LIFE AND EDUCATION

We are all shaped by early-life experiences. The events of childhood and adolescence color the ways in which we see and understand the world for the rest of our lives. While it would be reductive to believe that Harrison's later work was determined by her earliest experiences, there are some salient events that may well have colored her interpretations of Greek religion.

Perhaps the most crucial was the death of her mother one month after Harrison was born. Reportedly a very affectionate child, this must have impacted her profoundly. Children who have lost their mothers very early in life often have a conflicted view of the absent mother, unknown and unknowable. Since she is not present to hurt, scold, command, or reprimand them, they may idealize her or they may feel anger at her for having abandoned them, an anger that is often repressed and sublimated. The child may thus harbor overwhelmingly intense, ambivalent feelings about the dead parent whom she both idealizes and abhors.

But this trauma was all too soon followed by another. Her aunt Harriet, who came to live with Harrison and her father after the mother's death, stayed only until Harrison was five years old before leaving to marry. Harrison had loved this aunt and was greatly loved by her in return. She took the loss of this mother-substitute very hard.

Making the situation even more difficult, Jane's father soon thereafter took a new wife, Gemimi Meredith, a woman who

seems to have wasted little affection on Harrison. Nor did Jane care for this difficult woman, who proceeded to bear children with her father and bring new half-siblings into the family—children whom she unsurprisingly favored.

In these few events it is possible to see the outlines of Harrison's later fascination with the theme of the erased but still-potent goddesses. A beloved and idealized mother figure is replaced by later figures introduced by the father, figures undeserving of devotion.

Harrison's biographer, Sandra Peacock, connects Harrison's valorization of the mother and the feminine, and her attempts in adulthood to create a circle of sympathetic and like-minded people to replace the family that she lost in her childhood to these early events. Such episodes would lead to both her later rejection of the patriarchal religion of her childhood, even as she retained a strong sense of the numinous, and to her drive to excavate (both literally and metaphorically) the primacy of the goddess in the history of Greek religion.

Harrison's stepmother was committed to a stern Evangelical religion that did not at all suit Harrison's temperament. Although, given the secular intellectual climate of late nineteenth century England, the adult Harrison would very likely have had to struggle with her Christian faith in any case—her stepmother's imposition of her crude if fervent, anti-intellectual, dogmatic religion on the sensitive, questioning young girl must have influenced Harrison's mature disavowal of Christianity. This repudiation was rarely stated openly but is nevertheless evident throughout her writing.

Yet in other ways, her stepmother's Evangelical Christianity may have had a positive influence on her later attitudes toward religion in general:

> Evangelicalism combined rational, Calvinist nonconformity with a passionate, emotional sense of mystery and superstition. Gemimi Harrison [Harrison's stepmother] seems to have exhibited both traits. In everyday life, her compulsive propriety clashed with Jane's high spirits, but intellectually, her 'fervent semi-revivalist' faith stimulated

> her stepdaughter's imagination. Its effect became apparent decades later, when Jane turned her attention to the wild emotion of the Greek chthonic cults, Gemimi's religious fervor having contributed to her passion for the emotional element of religion. (Peacock 1988: 15)

While Harrison rejected the Christianity of her childhood, as did many intellectuals of the late nineteenth century, she seems to have retained a core understanding of "religious fervor"; a supra-rational passion often marginalized by the Anglican church's conservative religious forms. Harrison's childhood exposure to passionate, non-rational religious experience may have fostered her later sympathetic understanding of the mystery cults, despite her rejection of evangelical Christianity, an understanding not available through even the most scrupulous study of the literary texts and archeological remains of these cults.

Harrison's earliest education was in the hands of a series of governesses, as was typical for a girl of her social class at that time. One of these, she recalls, was

> a woman of real intelligence, ignorant but willing and eager to learn anything and everything I wanted. Together we learnt to read German, Latin badly ... the Greek Testament and even a little Hebrew ... Alas! my kind governess was shortly removed to a lunatic asylum. What share I may have had in her mental downfall I do not care to inquire. (Harrison 1926: 26–27)

On Sundays she "followed the prayers in Latin, and the lesson in German, and the Gospel in Greek" (1926: 19). Although Harrison greatly disparaged her "Victorian education [as] ingeniously useless" (1926: 22), her exposure to classical learning in her early years would be considered very remarkable today. (Over the course of her life she would eventually come to know seventeen languages). From 1867 to 1870 (ages sixteen to nineteen) she was sent to Cheltenham Ladies' College, an institution chosen by her stepmother for its strictly Evangelical orientation.

Figure 1.1. Jane Harrison as Alcestis, Oxford, 1877.

Harrison seems to have had a difficult time adjusting to school and being away from home. However, school had its advantages. The school's reform-minded headmistress, Dorothea Beale, was devoted to providing her young female charges with an education that was advanced for its day. Indeed, some parents considered Beale to be too intellectual (Peacock 1988: 26). From the first, Harrison stood out for her brilliance. This and her habit of rejecting friends had the effect of distancing her from the other girls. She initially formed a close friendship with headmistress Beale. However Harrison finally rejected her too after reading D. F. Strauss's *Life of Jesus* (1835), a book whose denial of Christ's divinity and its interpretation of Christ's miracles historically and mythically rather than supernaturally, shook her Christian faith (Peacock 1988: 28). Harrison's reading of Strauss's book marked a major turn in her intellectual life; its skepticism toward Christianity marks all of her later writings.

From 1874 to 1879, Harrison studied classics at Newnham College, one of the first women's colleges at Cambridge (see Figure 1.1). She was among the first women permitted to study at Cambridge, since Newnham had opened only in 1871. Here, freed from the company of men and the demands of family life, she was surrounded by other talented, intelligent women. She formed many new friendships, although she was also notorious for dropping friends. Her fellow students recognized her brilliance and were overawed by her. The communal life among scholarly women suited her well:

> If I had been rich I should have founded a learned community for women, with vows of consecration and a beautiful rule and habit; as it is, I am content to have lived many years of my life in a college. I think, as civilization advances, family life will become, if not extinct, at least much modified and curtailed. (Harrison 1926: 89)

In 1879 she sat for the classical Tripos and although she had received the highest mark in philosophy and the examiners debated between awarding her a first or a second, she was finally

awarded only a second. While this upset her, she only very rarely mentioned it. She attributed this disappointment to the disruption caused by her leaving Newnham for one term to care for her favorite stepsister Jessie, who was dying of an appendiceal abscess and scarlet fever. A second suggested reason was the emotional turmoil caused by a failed love affair with her Greek and Latin tutor, Henry Butcher; a relationship that in later years, she and Hope Mirrlees, her companion, attempted to keep secret (Peacock 1988: 52).

She left Cambridge in 1880 to teach Latin at Notting Hill High School, a girls' school in Oxford. After teaching there for one term she left for London to study Greek art and archeology at the British Museum with Sir Charles Newton, who had participated in the excavation of the Temple of Zeus at Olympia and was now the keeper of the Greek and Roman antiquities at the Museum. There, from 1880 to 1898, Harrison taught and lectured, mostly on Greek art. Her lectures were very well-attended and the response to them was enthusiastic.

Although Harrison is today most often remembered as a "ritualist," the study of ritual was not her principal interest at the outset of her post-university career. Instead, it was art history that provided the lens through which she began her exploration of Greek religion. Her London lectures and her first publications were analyses of Greek art. Her earliest attitude toward Greek art was that of idealization (fairly characteristic of the European intellectual attitude of the nineteenth century), seeing in the artworks of Greek antiquity, especially those attributed to Phidias, the embodiment of Platonic idealism, the realization of perfection similar to Platonic "forms."[1]

Robert Ackerman outlines Harrison's early approach to art as beginning with a somewhat naïve Platonic Idealism, which she had abandoned by 1890:

> A reader of her later work would turn hundreds of pages in vain to see a mention of the word "Ideality" with a capital "I," for she is no longer interested in it. In fact, her mature work may be thought of as a countermovement to the idealizing

> tendency that so clammily chills nearly every discussion of Greek art through the nineteenth century. Indeed, she never in any of her later work even gets to Phidias and the fifth century; her entire focus shifts to the Archaic age, and the statues that figure as illustrations are the early *korai* of the seventh and sixth centuries. (Ackerman 1991a: 75–76)

Harrison was later strongly influenced by Giovanni Morelli's art historical "revolution." Morelli had introduced the practice of authenticating artworks and identifying their creators by focussing on "apparently insignificant details of the treatment of minor features (earlobes, hands, eyebrows) which could identify a painter as reliably as his handwriting" (Beard 2000: 23). This seemingly obsessive attention to details would come to be a hallmark not only of Harrison's early study of art history but also her later study of Greek religion.[2]

In 1887, Harrison's close friend D. S. MacColl sent her a letter criticizing her style of lecturing, which made her furious. This led to Harrison's shift from art history to Greek religion and her life in the years immediately following the painful break with MacColl (until she joined Newnham College eleven years later in 1898) can be seen as dominated by what Henri Ellenberger calls a "creative illness."[3]

Nothing hurts like the truth. When MacColl, probably with some accuracy, criticized her lecturing style, which had been described as "overheated, sensationalistic and superficial" (Ackerman 1991a: 79), delivered in a high-pitched tone of voice, accompanied by numerous audio-visual accessories (very unusual for the time) she became enraged. "I tore [the letter] up in the fury of first reading, but unhappily that only made me remember every word of it" (Harrison, qtd. in Beard 2000: 58). After Harrison's initial angry reaction, she became abject and sank into a depression. She "quite decided ... to give up entirely next year all lecturing, because I see only too clearly that it is the ἐπιδεικτικὸς λόγος [i.e., 'display oratory'] that has been my undoing" (qtd. in Beard 2000: 58). Although she did not, in fact, abandon irrevocably her lecturing or her association with

MacColl, and she does not even seem to have given up the audiovisual tricks that evoked part of MacColl's criticism, this event did cause her to begin her trips to Greece and her archeological work with Dörpfeld. She describes her life as having collapsed and of then undergoing a kind of "mystical" experience, characteristic of the late phases of a creative illness. Her friend Jessie Stewart describes this period in Harrison's life as characterized by "depression, loneliness, a sense of disaster bringing a 'conviction of sin' [followed by] exaltation, peace, and joy, a new focus, a sensation of oneness" (qtd. in Ackerman 1991a: 79). The creative illness changed the direction of her life.

Without this precipitating event Harrison might have continued the rest of her life lecturing at the British Museum. Instead, she left England for Greece, got her hands dirty with the actual work of archeology—a neglected and derided pursuit at that time—and found the direction that she was to follow for the next thirty years: the excavation (both literal and metaphorical) of the earlier layers of Greek religion. Her period of "depression, loneliness, and disaster" appears to have ended during or after her 1888 visit to Greece. After this, her approach to Greek art was now combined with her interest in archeology and in the origins of Greek religion. Upon her return to England in 1890, this "new birth" resulted in two publications: her *Manual of Mythology in Relation to Greek Art* (a translation of Maxime Collignon's *Mythologie figureé de la Grèce*) and a long historical introduction to Margaret Verrall's translation of Book I of Pausanias' *Attica* (a section of his *Descriptions of Greece*). The translation and the introduction were published together as *Mythology and Monuments of Ancient Athens* (1890). In the preface to her translation of Collignon's *Manual of Mythology*, Harrison sets forth her new views:

> If we would know the truth about the origin of mythological types, it is to archaic art we must look,—to a time when the utterance of the artist, if sometimes rude and inarticulate, was always robust and sincere. Truth with the early artist comes even before beauty; as yet he works for a people whose faith is more developed than their senses.

> The study of mythography is in England yet in its infancy, but it may safely be prophesied that not many years will elapse before it becomes not only part of the advanced discipline of the classical scholar, but also an indispensable and attractive element in classical school teaching. M. Collignon's manual offers an admirable introduction to the study, and as no English handbook exists a translation was much needed. (qtd. in Ackerman 1991a: 80)

She was no longer lecturing at the British Museum and spent some of her time working in Athens on archeological projects. Her first major work, *Prolegomena to the Study of Greek Religion* (1991 [1903]), issued from this time of emotional turmoil and depression. *Prolegomena,* in its somewhat disorganized state, represents her tentative explorations of new ideas and radically new proposals about the earliest stages of Greek religion. It also reflects the process of a brilliant woman discovering her unique way of thinking and presenting it in her own unique voice.

Although Harrison had not yet in 1890 met Gilbert Murray, Francis Cornford, or A. B. Cook, in her Introductory Essay to Margaret Verrall's translation of Pausanias' *Mythology and Monuments of Ancient Athens,* she had already set out the general direction to be taken a little later by the "Cambridge Ritualists":

> I have tried everywhere to get at, where possible, the cult as the explanation of the legend. My belief is that in many, even in the large majority of cases, *ritual practice misunderstood* [her italics] explains the elaboration of myth ... Some of the loveliest stories the Greeks have left us will be seen to have taken their rise, not in poetic imagination, but in primitive, often savage, and, I think, always *practical* ritual. In this matter—in regarding the myth-making Greek as a practical savage rather than a poet or philosopher—I follow, *quam longo intervallo* [after how long a time], in the steps of Eusebius, Lobeck, Mannhardt, and Mr. Andrew Lang. (Verrall 1890: iii)

Here Harrison laid out one of the principles that guided so much of her future study of Greek religion, as well as that of the other Ritualists: since myth is often, as she said, "ritual practice misunderstood," the proper study of myth must aim at recovering what the primitives *did*, rather than what was later (often mistakenly) invented to explain what was done. That is, myths performed an "etiologic" function, providing explanations for older rituals whose origins, purposes, and functions had been forgotten.

Harrison had always been visually and aesthetically oriented in a field that was at that time decidedly text-centered.[4] She was now able, against firm opposition, to channel her visual and aesthetic talents into bringing the new findings from archeology into the field of classics. She brought the fields of archeology, art history, and aesthetics to bear upon this heretofore logocentric field. Beard cites a number of other factors that may have helped to expand Harrison's interests, noting that in 1879, just after Harrison finished her studies at Newnham College, the Tripos examinations were expanded beyond their former exclusive emphasis on language and translation to include art, archeology, ritual, and religious studies. It is not known exactly when Harrison became aware of these changes, but she would certainly have known about them when she returned there in 1898 to teach classics until 1922. (Although Harrison had received an excellent education in classical studies at Newnham, she persistently downplayed its importance, choosing instead to emphasize the importance of what she learned from her mentor in archeology, Wilhelm Dörpfeld.)

Many of Harrison's insights were dependent on contemporaneous archeological discoveries. Heinrich Schliemann's excavations of Troy and Mycenae occurred in the 1870s and Sir Arthur Evans's excavations at Knossos began in 1900. The uncovering of these sites of mythic fame radically altered how Europeans thought about Greek antiquity. Although sculptures and other objects had been turning up for centuries, with a big uptick beginning in the Renaissance, now suddenly, large numbers of physical objects were being discovered for study: entire cities, temples, buildings, sculptures, vases with exquisite paintings, the

famous "mask of Agamemnon" from Mycenae, epigraphs, coins, and many other objects.

Although we think of Harrison today as the central member of the group known as the Cambridge Ritualists, this name is an anachronism coming into use only in the 1960s, decades after Harrison's death in 1928 and her subsequent (temporary) eclipse in the academic world. The name was never employed by the members of the group themselves. Beard questions not only the appropriateness of the term, but even the existence of the "group" as such. She emphasizes that it is far from clear that the group we recognize today as the Cambridge Ritualists saw themselves as a coherently defined group with a common program. They were an association of friends and colleagues engaged in the more loosely defined common project of reforming the field of classical studies. They supported then-radical notion that rituals *preceded* their associated myths. The group was united by the conviction that ritual was earlier and more fundamental than myth.

Harrison often referred to herself in her personal correspondence with her friends Murray and Cornford (see Figure 1.2), and signed her letters to them, as "*Ker*," especially when overcome by strong negative emotions (Peacock 1988: 141, 175). She was comfortable identifying, even if somewhat playfully, with these sinister, often feminine entities. It is clear that Harrison identified with the *keres* and with the older chthonic goddesses that she saw as having been submerged by the *arriviste* male gods. Likewise, in her correspondence she often referred to Murray as "*Ther*" (beast); a term we may find hard to square with the buttoned-down image of this scholar that has been passed on to us.

After the publication of *Prolegomena* in 1903, Harrison made yet another sharp intellectual turn after reading the works of Henri Bergson, Émile Durkheim, and Sigmund Freud. Incorporating Bergson's philosophy, Durkheim's sociology, and Freud's psychology with her study of Greek religion, she proposed a radically new origin for ritual. In putting together *Themis* (1912), she declines to write about Greek tragedy in her own voice, instead including a section written wholly by Murray. She asked Francis Cornford to write Chapter 7 of *Themis*, "The Origin of the

Figure 1.2. Jane Harrison and (from left to right) Hugh Stewart, Gilbert Murray and Francis Cornford in the Malting House Garden, Cambridge.

Olympic Games." On one hand, she characteristically exhibits her warm intellectual generosity toward a member of the circle of ritualists, a group that she gathered around herself as the family of her adult life to replace the family she lost as a child. On the other hand, in deferring to a male author to write an important chapter in her own book, she silences and effaces herself in a way that harks back to more traditional feminine roles.

Among the great transformations of the nineteenth century were changes in the roles deemed acceptable for women of all social classes.[5] Harrison was one of the first women allowed to study at Cambridge. She achieved an astonishing degree of professional success in a world still overwhelmingly male-dominated, which must have rankled a woman as intelligent, capable, and self-willed as she. It is not hard to imagine Harrison's life experience reflected in her view of the history of Greek religion as a story of the feminine being overlaid by the masculine.

Beard sees the heroized Harrison we know today as the product of conscious creation by her former students, her friends and co-workers, and by Harrison herself. Because at some point Harrison burned most of her papers, we must often rely on only one side of her extensive correspondences, the letters she wrote that were retained by her friends and colleagues. Beard emphasizes how our current view of Harrison reflects the selective nature of the papers that were saved and those that were discarded or suppressed by her acquaintances. Of great importance in this regard is the acknowledged suppression of much of Harrison's personal story by her former student and life partner, Hope Mirrlees, who openly and repeatedly alluded to the fact that there were important elements of Harrison's personal life that she (Mirrlees) was suppressing. Mirrlees studied at Newnham, where she was Harrison's student from 1910 to 1913, and thereafter lived more or less constantly with Harrison until Harrison's death. In 1922, they moved together to Paris ("Paris Lesbos," as it was known at the time [Beard 2000: 139]). Numerous friends, acquaintances, authors, and biographers took it as common knowledge that Harrison and Mirrlees were lovers (or life partners, or "intimate friends"). This later focus on women friends and a woman life-partner echoes her scholarly

emphasis on female divinities and her (never quite explicit) affirmation of what an appreciation of the sacredness of the feminine energy they embody can mean to contemporary women.

NOTES

1. Harrison provides an illustration of her early Platonic, idealizing attitude toward Greek art in her preface to *Introductory Studies in Greek Art*:

    > The answer is, I believe, found in a certain peculiar quality of Greek art which adapts itself to the consciousness of successive ages, which has within it no seed of possible death,—a certain largeness and universality which outlives the individual race and persists for all time. The meaning of this quality, which we call Ideality, it is the sole object of this little book to develope [sic] ... The meaning of the term Ideality I have sought to explain by reference to the teaching of Plato. (1892: vi)

    Harrison's early understanding of art was also heavily reliant upon textual interpretation: "Greek literature is the best and only sound comment on Greek art: what is expressed but undefined in Phidias becomes clearly articulate in Plato. The language of words is more distinct than the language of art." (1892: vi)

    In her later work, she abandons not only the idealizing approach to art, but her early reliance on the textual interpretation of art. Instead, she comes to trust her own aesthetic sense, her interpretation, her sharp eye for detail.
2. Giovanni Morelli (1816–1891) developed a method of evaluating artworks by paying very close attention to small details, such as the individual folds in ears, especially in lesser figures in a given painting, as opposed to larger scale effects such as subject matter and composition. He published this technique in 1890 as *Die Werke Italienischer Meister* (*The Works of the Italian Masters*), which was translated into English in 1893. Morelli had studied medicine in Switzerland and Germany and had taught anatomy at the University of Munich before turning his attention to art analysis. His background in anatomy, with its careful attention to minute detail of the human body, may lie behind his novel approach to art.

    Harrison took up the Morellian method enthusiastically, a copy of his work accompanying her on her travels (Beard: 23). This method of evaluating artworks runs through Harrison's later works, *Prolegomena* and *Themis*, so much so that it becomes characteristic of her work.
3. Ellenberger identifies the "creative illness" that afflicts many highly creative individuals at some point in their lives, drawing his primary

examples from the field of psychiatry, include Antoine Mesmer, Friedrich Nietzsche, Sigmund Freud (from 1894 to 1900), and C. G. Jung (from 1913 to 1919). He describes this creative illness as a mental and emotional disturbance that:

> ... is to be found among shamans, among mystics of various religions, in certain philosophers and creative writers ... A creative illness succeeds a period of intense preoccupation with an idea and search for a certain truth. It is a polymorphous condition that can take the shape of depression, neurosis, psychosomatic ailments, or even psychosis. Whatever the symptoms, they are felt and painful, if not agonizing, by the subject, with alternating periods of alleviation and worsening. Throughout the illness the subject never loses the thread of his dominating preoccupation. It is often compatible with normal, professional activity and family life. But even if he keeps to his social activities, he is almost entirely absorbed within himself. He suffers from feelings of utter isolation, even when he has a mentor who guides him through the ordeal (like the shaman apprentice with his master). The termination is often rapid and marked by a phase of exhilaration. The subject emerges from his ordeal with a permanent transformation in his personality and the conviction that he has discovered a great truth or a new spiritual world. (Ellenberger 1970: 447–48)
>
> This is how Mesmer came to proclaim the truth of animal magnetism ... Nietzsche the eternal return, Freud the Oedipus complex and the infantile sexual root of neurosis, and Jung the anima and the process of individuation. (Ellenberger 1970: 890)

It was in her creative illness that Harrison came upon her new understanding of Greek religion.

4. To give but one example of such text-centeredness: Nietzsche's *Birth of Tragedy*, considered so radical a revisioning of Greek culture at the time, was yet focussed almost exclusively on the writings of poets, tragedians, and philosophers.
5. Accompanying these social changes in the status of women were a number of fin-de-siècle cultural phenomena centering on women and the cult of eroticism, a large, almost obsessive subject among (male) artists and thinkers of the time. Images of femme fatales, such as such as Salome and Judith holding the heads of John the Baptist and Holofernes, became frequent in the arts. Another form of the femme fatale, the female vampire, came to dominate at this time (vampires having previously been seen predominantly as male). Depictions of female water spirits such as Undines, Sirens, Banshees, Naiads, Lorelei, nixies, mermaids, and Rusalkas became prominent in literature, music, and art. "Another

conspicuous theme was the cult of the prostitute: artists such as Toulouse-Lautrec and Klimt painted these women with a certain fondness; writers such as De Maupassant, Wedekind, Wildgans, and Popper-Lynkeus glorified them" (Ellenberger 1970: 283).

This was the time when Freud undertook his investigation into hysteria, the great psychic ailment of women of the age. Later in this period Jung discovered the "anima," the feminine element in the male psyche. Jung understood femme fatale images as manifestations of "negative anima."

It is against this background that Harrison began to unearth not only the earliest Greek goddesses in their terrible splendor, but also the *keres*, the predominantly female spirits of sickness, famine, and death (to be examined in Chapter 2).

CHAPTER 2
THE BIRTH OF THE GODDESS

CONTRIBUTIONS FROM ART

As we have already noted, although after completing her studies at Newnham College Harrison was supremely qualified to teach, she was denied a position there. Instead, she moved to London and spent nearly twenty years from 1880 to 1898 working at the British Museum. There, she delivered a series of very popular and well-attended lectures on Greek art and archeology. This occurred at a time when archeology as a field was just becoming established, with amateur archeologists such as Heinrich Schliemann and Sir Arthur Evans[1] making their spectacular discoveries. Harrison's aesthetic approach to the ancient Greek world, which incorporated the findings of archeology, was very new and eagerly received by the public, though not by established classicists. Harrison was among the very first to incorporate the findings of art and archeology into her lectures, and writing at a time when archeology was, incredibly to us, held in disdain by established academics.

One of Harrison's greatest contributions to the study of Greek religion was her demonstration through the close study of art and archeological finds that the depictions in art (predominantly vase paintings) often contradicted the versions of myths and rituals presented in surviving Greek literature, principally the Homeric epics and the tragedies. These discrepancies led her to raise questions about the given understanding of the relation between myths and rituals. Art and literature, she thought, might

represent diverging expressions derived from an earlier common tradition, perhaps including lost epics from the Homeric cycle and other now-lost mythic literature. In his funeral address for Harrison, Murray explains Harrison's turn toward ritual as follows:

> [W]e must escape from the tyranny of the fully articulate and finished literary accounts, and wring a deeper and truer evidence from the inarticulate and half-understood rituals which the Greeks really practiced. We must study the things done at festivals ... and discover the stuff of religion before theology. (G. Murray, *Jane Ellen Harrison: An Address*, 4–5, qtd. in Beard 2000: 4)

While Harrison's revised understanding of Greek myth and ritual were made most evident in her later books *Prolegomena* and *Themis*, they were nascently present in her earlier writings: the books *Myths of the Odyssey in Art and Literature* (1882) and *Introductory Studies in Greek Art* (1892), as well as the introductory essay and commentary in the book she wrote in collaboration with Margaret Verrall: *Mythology and Monuments of Ancient Athens: Being a Translation of a Portion of the Attica of Pausanias* (1890).

Anticipating Freud and later post-modernism, Harrison was intent on discerning an earlier stage of Greek religion that later art and literature had attempted to conceal. At roughly the same time Freud was beginning to work out his ideas (but before reading any of his work), Harrison was pursuing a project in Greek religion analogous to what Freud was doing with his patients: unearthing the unseen, bringing to consciousness that which has been suppressed. In neither field is such suppression ever entirely successful or complete. In her attempt to recover the lost religion and its rituals Harrison had necessarily to engage in speculation. She had to "see" what no longer was, as, of course, did Freud.

For Harrison, the process of evolution in Greek religion was, at least until the re-emergence of earlier religious elements in the mystery religions of later Antiquity, an unfortunate, negative process of falsification, beautification, and "taming" of the earlier

religion dominated by dark chthonic forces: represented by daemonic spirits known as *keres,* Harpies, Gorgons, and Sirens as well as by animals like serpents, wolves, and owls. A religion of such terrifying forces recalls E. B. Tylor's unseen animism of weather, fertility, animals, places, springs, mountains, rivers, and trees (Bošković 2021: 56–57, 92; Ackerman 1991a: 36–39).[2]

Throughout her writing Harrison evokes the theme that much of the surviving Greek literature, beautiful as it is, represents a falsification and betrayal of this earlier Greek religion. Primitive Greek religion, Harrison believed, was dominated by apotropaic rituals dedicated to averting these terrifying, unseen forces. She believed that this evolutionary transformation of religion was led by artists, who gave the previously inchoate forces first their theriomorphic (animal) appearances, then anthropotheriomorphic (combined animal and human), and finally beautifully anthropomorphic appearances; a progressive evolutionary process, finally tending toward beautification and "euphemism." This process was later continued by poets who attributed personalities to these now fully anthropomorphized gods and goddesses, assigned to them delimited, departmentalized powers, and inserted them into a patriarchal family structure reflecting the familial structure of contemporary Greek society. Harrison claimed that the Greeks had a natural abhorrence of the ugly and that their later art possessed the tendency toward beautification (with the notable exception of Gorgons and Medusa, as discussed below). These themes and ideas, which were first articulated in her early writings, came to fruition in *Prolegomena.*

A fine example of Harrison's use of artistic evidence to suggest an alternative understanding of a literary myth is her discussion of the Judgment of Paris. Even more compelling is her tracing of the evolution of goddesses from the formless, aniconic forces and spirits to theriomorphic, then anthropotheriomorphic, and finally to beautiful, very humanlike deities. In this process, she describes the parallel evolution and transformation of Greek religion from one originally centered on rituals designated to propitiate unseen physical forces, Underworld deities, and the

ancestors to one focused on service (tendance) of the Olympian gods and goddesses.

REVISION OF A MYTH

The earliest extant literary evidence of the myth of the Judgment of Paris is a brief mention in the *Iliad* (24:25–30) as well as in references to the *Cypria* (part of the now-lost Epic Cycle), followed by later, more elaborate tellings by Ovid, Lucian, Pseudo-Apollodorus, and Hyginus. Harrison believed that this myth, which artificially forces together and trivializes the three Olympian goddesses Hera, Athene, and Aphrodite, displaces an earlier motif of three identical maiden figures such as the *Charites*. The later myth individualizes and differentiates the three maidens as distinct goddesses. She views this literary myth as a "degrad[ation of] the story into a beauty-contest between three thoroughly personal goddesses, vulgar in itself and complicated by bribery still more vulgar" (Harrison 1991: 298). Adducing evidence from vase paintings that had until then been understood as depicting the Judgment of Paris story, Harrison showed that on all but one of them the story depicted was in fact that of Hermes leading the *Charites*, bringers of gifts to humankind.

She demonstrates that the three goddesses in the paintings cannot for the most part be differentiated from one another (see Figure 2.1). In most of the examined paintings the three figures are not identifiable as Aphrodite, Hera, or Athene (although in some Athene can be identified by her helmet). In many, the three female figures are identical. The apple is often absent, however even when it is present the goddesses often hold other fruits or flowers as well. Paris, too, is frequently entirely absent from the depictions of the story of which he is supposedly the center. When he is present he sometimes peripheral or small (see Figure 2.2).

In one painting Paris holds a veil before his face, shielding himself from the goddesses (see Figure 2.3), while in another he is attempting to flee, restrained by Hermes from doing so (see Figure 2.4).

Figure 2.1. Hermes with Paris and the Three Goddesses.

Figure 2.2. Hermes with Paris and the Three Goddesses.

Figure 2.3. Paris veiling his face before the Three Goddesses and Hermes.

Figure 2.4. Hermes restrains Paris fleeing the Goddesses. Work in public domain.

Harrison proposes that the myth depicted in the vase paintings is an older one, far older than the literary myth that over time replaced it: "'Did not the [literary] myth itself in some sense rise out of the already existing art form, an art form in which Paris had no place, in which the golden apple was not?' That form was the ancient myth of Hermes leading the three Korai or Charites" (1991: 297). She goes on to suggest elements that may have been part of the earlier myth:

> From vases alone it would be sufficiently evident, I think, that the 'Judgment of Paris' is really based on Hermes and the Charites ... The Κρίσις, the Decision, of Paris is always as much a Choice as a Judgment ... The particular decision is associated in legend with the name of a special hero, of one particular 'young man moving to and fro alone, in an empty hut in the

> firelight.'... And what exactly has the young man to decide? Which of the three is fairest? Or whose gifts he desires the most? It matters not at all, for both are different ways of saying the same thing ... early versions scarcely distinguish the goddesses from the gifts they bring. There is no difference between them except the difference of their gifts. They are Charites, Gift-bringers. They are their own gifts. Or, as the Greek put it, their gifts are their σημεῖα [semeia], their tokens. And Hermes had led them long since, in varying forms, before the eyes of each and all of mankind. They might be conceived as undifferentiated, as mere Givers-of-Blessing in general. But it needed only a little reflection to see that Χάρις [Charis: meaning grace, favor, or kindness] often wars against Χάρις, and that if one be chosen, others must be rejected. (1991: 298)

Harrison has identified the problem—the misalignment between myth and art—but wisely has not given a final answer as to its resolution, instead pointing to the need for further study and the search for further evidence.

EVOLUTION OF GODDESSES FROM KERES

Among Harrison's most significant contributions to the study of Greek religion is her radically new theory about the origins of the Greek goddesses (theagony) and, to a lesser extent, the origins of the Greek gods (theogony), again based on her close examination of vase paintings. Over the course of five chapters in *Prolegomena* (Chapters III through VII) she posits a framework for understanding the prehistory of goddesses and gods. This evolutionary process for goddesses (but not for gods) begins with unseen, formless terrors, emotional forces whose presence inspired rites of purgation, purification, and aversion:

> [I]t is only by a somewhat severe mental effort that we realize the fact essential to our study that *there were no gods at all*, that what we have to investigate is not so many actual

> facts and existences but only conceptions of the human mind that conceived them. Art which makes the image, literature which crystallizes attributes and functions, arrest and fix this shifting kaleidoscope; but, until the coming of art and literature and to some extent after, the formulary of theology is 'all things are in flux' (πάντα ῥεῖ). (1991: 164)

Formless terrors ("conceptions") evolve into "vague, shifting outlines as ghosts and sprites, later crystallized into clear shapes as goddesses and gods" (1991: 162).

Harrison devotes a lengthy chapter to the *keres,* sinister spiritual entities ("sprites"), that she sees as representing a middle stage in the evolution of the goddesses (but again, not of the male gods).

The *keres* emerge as embodiments of the earlier inchoate, aniconic terrors, and only much later evolve into the fully formed, anthropomorphic goddesses: "The first necessity is that by an effort of the sympathetic imagination we should think back the 'many' [goddesses] we have so sharply and strenuously divided, into the haze of the primitive 'one'" (1991: 164). Since Harrison does not define this primitive "one," we are left to wonder whether she means by this a single, primordial goddess, a unitary emotional state, or some other single, heretofore undescribed *mysterium* [mystery]. It is unlikely that she means a single goddess since she has notified us just previously that "*there were no gods at all.*" By speaking of "one," Harrison may have fallen into her own trap. She argues against the modern habit of separation, distinction, classification: "It may even happen, as in the case of the Olympian divinities, that articulation and discrimination sound the note of approaching decadence" (1991: 164). By tracing back the sharply defined "many" (the Olympian deities) to a "primitive 'one'" she may have committed the very error she is decrying: a "one" is as sharply defined as a "many." This inhibits our ability to describe an unseen, primordial *mysterium* that is neither one nor many, but which precedes both and encompasses all possibilities without enumerating or describing them.

The *keres* are distinct from *daimones.* A *daimon* is a supernatural agent of unexpected, intrusive events in a person's life. Unlike *keres,* which are always evil (Hornblower 2003: 806), *daimones* may be bringers of either good or evil fortune. Homer and other earlier poets sometimes referred to the Olympian gods as *daimones,* but *daimones* were more often considered in non-anthropomorphic terms, as were *the keres.* The *daimones* were originally "unpredictable, anonymous, and often frightful manifestations. Accordingly, the adjective *daimonios* meant 'strange,' 'incomprehensible,' 'uncanny'" (Hornblower 2003: 426). Over time, *daimones* became personal guardians and could bring either good luck or harm. In later antiquity, the *daimones* became guardian spirits who accompanied humans not only during life but after as well. Originally intermediary between gods and humans, they later become equivalent to the Olympian gods (as they were for Homer). Later still, Christians separated the good *daimones* from the evil ones, interpreting the good *daimones* as angels and the evil *daimones,* which now included the Olympian gods, as wholly evil *demons.*

Like Max Müller,[3] Harrison saw personification as the origin of myth. For Harrison the emergence of the *keres* marks only the visualization of previously invisible, inchoate terrors. She saw the *keres* as representing all human fears: "[g]host, bacillus, disease, death-angel, death-fate, fate, bogey, magician" (1991: 212).

In Harrison's view, the Greeks had always understood the malevolent forces to be personal forces. Rather, the coming of the *keres* represented only a shift of identity from invisible to visible:

> It is commonly said that diseases are 'personified' by the Greeks. This is to invert the real order of primitive thought. It is not that a disease is realized as a power and then turned into a person, it is that primitive man seems unable to conceive of any force except as resulting from some person or being or sprite, something a little like himself. (1991: 168–69)

Keres embodied the destructive power of fire and of winds, the diseases and blights of plants, nightmares, and evil daydreams. Harrison attributes the objectification of *keres* to the artists, who in their vase-paintings, sculptures, and grave reliefs gave physical form to these previously unseen, formless entities. Makers of horror films have long known that our greatest fear is that of the unseen; monsters and the murderers are most frightening when they are never shown; monsters depicted on-screen become less terrifying, more manageable (even, at times, laughable). Similarly, by making the *keres* visibly perceptible the early Greek vase-painters made them less fearsome and more controllable. By giving them a body, the artists localized them and limited them. If the *ker* has a body, it cannot be everywhere, but only where its body is at a given moment. Moreover, very early depictions of the *keres* show them to be small, misshapen humanoid creatures, mildly unattractive child-like beings fluttering about with dragonfly wings. How fearful could such pitiful creatures be?

Harrison sees such early nameless *keres* as the ancestors of the later, more fully developed beings: Harpies and wind-demons, succubi, Sirens, Gorgons, Sphinxes, and Erinyes. Some of the *keres* probably originated as spirits of the dead, both male and female. Later embodiments of the *keres*, all feminine, became the ancestors of goddesses, according to Harrison. These figures, partway along the evolutionary line from *keres* to goddesses, include the *Semnai Theai* and the *Eumenides*.

EVOLUTION OF GODDESSES FROM UNSEEN TO ANIMAL AND HUMAN FORM

In her studies of vase paintings and funerary monuments, Harrison identified as *keres* many of the earliest visualized embodiments of dead ancestors. Indeed, it is as such ancestors that *keres* make their first appearance. These *keres* are depicted anthropomorphically. They will later be seen as manifestations of old age, as the causes of sickness, and of death itself. The *keres* of murdered kin are avenging *keres* of a different order: the Erinyes.

Figure 2.5. Herakles slaying "Geras," the Ker of Old Age.

The earliest depictions of a death *ker* lacks wings, appearing only as a sick old man, bent with age (1991: 174) (see Figure 2.5).

In Homer, the *ker* of the fate of death is no longer a small, harmless-appearing, genderless humanoid fluttering about on its dragonfly wings. There the *Ker* is female, a strong woman-like figure, cloaked in human blood, drawing men dead and alive off to their fates.

GORGONS AND MEDUSA

By far the most terrifying *keres* were the Gorgons. According to Harrison, Gorgon was originally a single chthonic deity, who later developed into a triple form, the three Gorgon sisters, by the general Greeks predilection for feminine triads such as the *Charites*, Graces, Fates, and the Horae (Seasons or Hours).

Harrison states that the Medusa was originally a bodiless head, only later acquiring a body (1991: 187). The head was a terrifying mask used in ritual, this mask being an embodiment of terror itself. The mask's function was apotropaic, employed on tombs, shields, ovens, and in temples (see Figure 2.6).

The power of the "ugly face" lay not only in its general ugliness, its snaky hair, and in its gaping mouth with its fangs and protruding tongue, but resided most prominently in its eye, precursor of the "evil eye" found throughout the Mediterranean world even today. Harrison suggests that Medusa's head was probably not yet gendered:

> [S]he is in fact the ugly bogey-, Erinys-side of the Great Mother; she is a potent goddess, not as in later days a

Figure 2.6. Gorgon mask governing outside of outdoor oven.

> monster to be slain by heroes. The highest divinities of the religion of fear and riddance became the harmful bogeys of the cult of 'service' [that is, Olympian religion]. (1991: 194)

The later-developed myth of Perseus as slayer of the Medusa is an attempt to control and transfer her power to the male hero. Medusa was originally a local chthonic goddess, seen as a terrifying mask, a head, an ugly face possessing power that could be employed apotropaically. Medusa was only later given a name, sisters, and myths to explain her origin and her downfall.

In her early work *Introductory Studies to Greek Art* (1892), Harrison (perhaps anachronistically) attributes the process of beautification characteristic of Greek art—exemplified in the transformation of the Gorgon Medusa into a beautiful woman—to the "idealism" of Plato's philosophy. However, after 1890 Harrison made a radical break with the idealistic and Platonic attitudes toward Greek art seen in her earliest works. Her idealism disappears. Plato and the literature and artworks of the fifth century become much less prominent as she delves more deeply into the darker, chthonic aspects of Greek religion and myth.

HARPIES, SIRENS, SPHINXES, ERINYES

Harrison sees the *keres* as developing into a large number of female beings. She sees the Harpies (from *harpazo*, to snatch away, to carry off) as deriving from the wind *daimones*. The *keres* associated with the hot, deadly winds become the Harpies that brought drought and famine by snatching away humankind's food, then spoiling and polluting it (see Figures 2.7. and 2.8.).

However, even as the Harpies brought death and carried away the souls of the dead, they also brought life by impregnating women and mares. They were at once both child-snatchers and child-nurturers; yet another manifestation of ambivalence characteristic of divine figures. The principle of ambivalence also applies to the associations of male and female gender, and life and death. Just as the female wind Harpies are associated with both life-bringing and life-taking, so the male Boreads may be

Figure 2.7. Harpies, the "Snatchers."

Figure 2.8. Harpy of gentle appearance carrying off the spirit of a dead child.

associated not only with death and killing but also with phallic, life-creating energy.

The principle of ambivalence applies to physical appearance as well. In early vase-paintings the Harpies had at times a sympathetic appearance, as when they were carrying the spirits of children, either at death or conception (1991: 177) (see Figure 2.8) but usually the Harpies were horrifying in appearance (see Figure 2.9). In some early depictions of the Gorgon she appears as a Harpy, suggesting that at a nascent stage, Gorgons and Harpies were closely related. Yet by the classical age (approximately fifth century), she has become a beautiful woman.

Harrison reminds us that although the Sirens appear in the *Odyssey*, Homer gives us no physical description of them. He tells us only that they drew men to their death by offering them knowledge:

> [i]t is strange and beautiful that Homer should make the Sirens appeal to the spirit, not to the flesh. To primitive man, Greek or Semite, the desire to know—to be as the

Figure 2.9. Harpy having the face of a Gorgon.

> gods—was the fatal desire ... Four points in the story of Homer must be clearly noted. The Sirens, though they sing to mariners, are *not* sea-maidens; they dwell on an island in a flowery meadow. They are mantic creatures like the Sphinx with whom they have much in common, knowing both the past and the future. Their song takes effect at mid-day, in a windless calm. The end of that song is death. It is only from the warning of Circe that we know of the heap of bones, corrupt in death—horror is kept in the background, seduction to the fore. (1991: 198–99)

The sirens are seductive Earth-born deities possessing prophetic powers of knowledge, who exhibit this power at midday. Their promise of god-like knowledge leads to death because their promised knowledge *is* the knowledge of death.

The Harpies, Sirens, and Sphinxes are all femme fatale *Ker* figures; female figures who seize men and drag them away to their deaths. Because they are female, even when they are repulsive in appearance there always remains a hint of erotic seduction (for men).

Harrison illustrates this process of anthropomorphism and beautification in *Myths of the Odyssey* where she tracks the evolution of the Sirens. As noted, Homer gives no physical description of the Sirens in the *Odyssey*; the depictions that have come down to us come exclusively from artists such as vase painters. While the earliest representations of the Sirens were of harpy-like "bird-women," they become increasingly anthropomorphic and more beautiful, until eventually they are lovely women resembling the Muses (see Figure 2.10).

For the Greeks, the Sirens were not mermaids, the fish-tailed marine creatures they have become for us. They were bird-women and "the bird-woman became a death-demon, a soul sent to fetch a soul, a Ker that lures a soul, a Siren" (1991: 201). Harrison saw that the Sirens are daughters of the Earth because they are the souls of the dead, buried in the Earth. These *keres* are not only the bringers of death and the carriers of the souls after death, but they are also themselves the souls of the dead.

Figure 2.10. Sirens witnessing a Satyr pursuing a Maenad.

Harrison shows how as the Sirens became increasingly beautiful in Hellenistic art, so in the Orphic cults and in neo-Platonism they became ever less fearful. They are no longer drawing us to a feared death, but rather the spirits we hope to become after death (see Figure 2.11).

Harrison further claims that the image of the winged, male love-god Eros of late antiquity evolved from a *Ker,* an evolution that involved a change of gender (1991: 207) as well as a progressive divinization, euphemization, and beautification of the *keres* of death.

Another lethal female descendant of the *keres* is the Sphinx (whose name means "choker, throttler"), another uncanny being representing a waypoint on the evolutionary road from formless terror to *ker* to goddess, but who never quite became a goddess. Although not described as physically beautiful, the Sphinx attracts by promising access to secret, mantic wisdom but then kills those whom she attracts.

Many of the primordial divinities Harrison discusses lack proper names, but are known rather by descriptive, attributive or adjectival names. These include *Erinyes* (the Angry Ones), the *Potniae* (the Awful or Powerful Ones), the *Maniae* (the Madnesses), the *Praxidikae* (the Vengeful Ones), the *Semnai Theae* (the Venerable Goddesses), and the *Eumenides* (the Kindly Ones).

Figure 2.11. Sirens with Odysseus and his crew.

It was the poets who gave these heretofore unseen and unseeable beings their appearance. Whereas in Homeric epic the *Erinyes* are unseen, in *The Eumenides* Aeschylus describes them as on one hand, loathly like the Gorgons but lacking their hideous masks, and on the other hand similar to the Harpies but lacking wings. They are black and terrible to see, but it is in their eyes that much of their power resides. Yet in vase paintings, the *Erinyes* are shown as lovely females, sometimes with wings like those of the Harpies but often without. They were always female and frequently depicted with a snake, reflecting their chthonic power.

In later Greek antiquity, the nature of the *Erinyes* was changed by vase painters and poets and in the Orphic cult:

> From the august ministers of the vengeance of the dead they have sunk to be the mere pitiless tormentors of hell. They lash on Sisyphos to his ceaseless task, they bind Peirithoös, they fasten Ixion to the wheel ... The criminals whom Justice (Dike)—the Orphic divinity of purification rather than vengeance—rejects as altogether incurable are pursued by an Erinys, 'the third and most savage of the ministrants of Adrasteia.' She drives them down into a place which Plutarch very properly describes as 'not to be seen, not to be spoken of.' The Erinyes are from beginning to end of the old order, implacable, vindictive; they know nothing of Orphic penance and purgatory; as 'angels of torment' they go to people a Christian Hell. (1991: 232)

Knowing Harrison's hostility to the Christianity of her youth, we can feel her outrage at the demotion of these horrifying, powerful goddesses to tormentors in a place that anticipates the "Christian Hell." Harrison perceives a persistent effort on the part of poets, artists, and philosophers to sanitize the Erinyes, first by depicting them in vase paintings without hideous appearance and later by demoting them from all-powerful *daimones* of vengeance to minor hellions. She insists: "Erinyes are from beginning to end of the old order, implacable, vindictive" (1991: 232).

The *Eumenides* were originally an entirely separate trinity of divinities local to Argos and other cities, but unknown at Athens. The *Semnai Theai* (the Venerable Goddesses) were local divinities of Athens, also distinct from the *Erinyes*. The *Semnai Theai* were sought out for fertile breezes and for the blessings of a fertile marriage.

THEORIES FOR THE ORIGIN OF THE GODDESS

Harrison presents divergent accounts of the emergence of the goddesses. Her account of how the goddesses arose from the *keres,* which were always multiple, has already been discussed. She also suggests that the goddesses first appeared in animal form but elsewhere she suggests that the apparent multiplicity of goddesses reflects merely the various names by which the one goddess was known in different localities, the Goddess in fact always and everywhere being only one. But then she also proposes that the goddess pantheon arose by way of the doubling and tripling of the one primordial goddess. Harrison left these apparent contradictions unaddressed.

There are problems with Harrison's suggestion that the goddesses emerged from *keres* and so were multiple from the beginning. The later-developed pantheon of goddesses includes no goddesses of dead ancestors, disease, winds, or famine. Instead, the poets assigned familial relations to the goddesses: mother, sister, wife, daughter.

According to Harrison goddesses arose from theriomorphic ancestresses such as snakes and birds. As they became anthropomorphic, they often retained their former animal selves as attributes such as Athene's owl. The Goddess was often nameless mistress of the animals:

> The Earth-Mother and each and every local nymph was mother not only of man but of all creatures that live; she is the 'Lady of the Wild Things' (πότνια θηρῶν) ... we can give the goddess no proper name. We call her rightly the Great

> Mother and the 'Lady of the Wild Things,' but farther we cannot go. She has been named Artemis and Cybele, but for neither name is there a particle of evidence. (1991: 264–66)

Because the Great Mother was mother of the Earth she was also the goddess of the dead, buried ancestors (1991: 266). As goddess of the living she was *Kourotrophos* ("rearer of children") (1991: 267).

Harrison thus suggests that Hera was originally a cow and Aphrodite a dove. Athene was originally the diver bird and the owl, the latter a bird that still haunts the Athenian Acropolis. Athene was also a serpent, an animal said to inhabit the Parthenon in antiquity. The serpent abandoned it, according to Herodotus, only when the city was about to be overrun by the Persians (1991: 305; Herodotus 2013: 546).

When Harrison speaks of the goddess as primordial, she speaks of her as being alone; there are no other goddesses and no associated god. According to this theory each goddess is truly "the" goddess, differing only by the location in which she is worshipped. In Athens the goddess was Athene, taking her name from the land. Hera reigned in splendid isolation as the goddess of Boeotia, Argos, and Samos. As the Greeks of one location, with their single goddess, came into contact with the people in other places, both Greek and non-Greek, these foreign goddesses were sometimes perceived as distinct from their own local goddess and were adopted and revered in their own right alongside the indigenous goddess. The interface of two or more such goddesses would bring into view subtle differences of identity and powers, which the later poets would then exaggerate. Some goddesses became less well-defined divine beings such as the Nymphs or Muses, while others became mortals, the human characters in myths. Some goddesses, such as *Ananke* (necessity) or *Peitho* (persuasion) were never represented visually, known only by their epithets. Still other goddesses, whose identities had been merged with that of another goddess, survived only as one of the many epithets applied to the single goddess: e.g., *Athêne Parthenos, Athêne Promachos, Athêne Nike, Athêne Ergane,*

Athêne Polias. Each of these "aspects" of Athene (virgin goddess, war goddess, victory goddess, goddess of workers, goddess of the city, respectively) may have originally been distinct goddesses.

Over time, the goddesses of the pantheon acquired distinct identities, most frequently through the work of poets who assigned to each of the goddesses' family relations, personalities, and departmentalized powers. In creating these family relationships, Homer and later poets imposed the patriarchal structure of their own world upon the goddesses and so placed them in a Zeus-dominated pantheon.

Finally, Harrison suggests the alternative origin of the pantheon of goddesses as arising by multiplication of a given goddess, separating out her different life stages, maiden, mother, and crone, and by recognizing her different functions, mother of the wild things, grain mother, warrior. But no matter which version of the "origin of the goddess" she was putting forward, Harrison recognized that eventually she was plural and subservient.

Surprisingly, Harrison did not view this demotion of the Feminine in entirely negative terms. In her view, the transition from the dominance of the primordial goddesses and feminine magic to the domination of the male gods was a necessary and beneficial development, accompanying the recognition of the fact of masculine strength. In Harrison's view, the move from matriarchy to patriarchy was a necessary and positive step (a view she shared with Bachofen), correlative with the rise of the polis. Yet centuries later in antiquity, there occurred a transition back to the Feminine, expressive of the recognition of the need by men as well as women for access to the energy associated with the feminine through participation in the female mystery cults, particularly the Eleusinian Mysteries.

> [T]he shift from matriarchy to patriarchy, and the shift itself, spite [sic] of a seeming retrogression, is a necessary stage in a real advance. Matriarchy gave women a false because [sic] a magical prestige. With patriarchy came inevitably the facing of a real fact, the fact of the greater natural weakness of women. Man the stronger, when

> he outgrew his belief in the magical potency of woman, proceeded by a pardonable practical logic to despise and enslave her as the weaker. The future held indeed a time when the non-natural, mystical truth came to be apprehended, that the stronger had a need, real and imperative, of the weaker. Physically nature had from the outset compelled a certain recognition of this truth, but that the physical was a sacrament of the spiritual was a hard saying, and its understanding was not granted to the Greek, save here and there where a flicker of the truth gleamed and went through the vision of philosopher or poet. (1991: 285)

Harrison sees the Greek poets as responsible for the goddesses' diminishment. It was they who made the goddesses into the daughters, wives, sisters, and mothers of the more recently arrived male gods. The stories the poets told about the complex interactions within this newly formed divine family resulted in the goddesses acquiring distinct, complex personalities. She singled out Hesiod as the worst of the poet mythologizers, but Homer, the author of the Homeric Hymns, and even the tragedians were not spared her scorn. The manifold powers associated with each of the individual goddesses were diminished and restricted so that they did not overlap with those of other goddesses or gods. As the goddesses' personalities became more human-like and more clearly defined they became ever less worthy of respect. The poets' myths had the goddesses, as well as the gods, engaging in behaviors that would be considered reprehensible in humans. In the hands of the poets, Hera became a shrewish, nagging wife. Aphrodite became a vengeful flirt, a femme fatale. Pandora was reduced to being the troublesome bringer of all evils. Against this, Harrison suggests that the jar from which Pandora (herself an early goddess, her name meaning "All Gifts") released the *keres* was a grave *pithos* used for burials, rather than a gift from Prometheus (1991: 169–70).

Harrison saw that the poets' project of humanizing the goddesses would be only temporarily successful. The poets' assignment of family relations, personalities, and limited purviews to

the individual goddesses diminishes them, making them small and "all too human." However, in her view the numinosity and power of the primordial goddess was preserved in the mystery cults such as those of Eleusis and Dionysos.

THE BIRTH OF THE GOD

Harrison's account in *Prolegomena* of theogony, the birth of the male gods, is radically different. Her account of the origins of the goddesses reads as compellingly alive, feeling as though it emerges from her deepest self-understanding. In contrast, in her account of the origins of the gods, the male gods of the invading Achaeans are superimposed clumsily on the cults of the pre-existing heroes worshipped by the indigenous Pelasgians. These newly arrived gods lack deep cultural roots, they are inauthentic and unconvincing. They are a disappointment.

Harrison claims that the earliest, indigenous gods originated as local heroes, mere mortal men who had died, rather than as attempts to contain the formless terrors that pervaded the primitive world as she believed the goddesses to be.[4] The heroes' tombs were associated with the serpent, reflecting the chthonic power of the hero; the grave site of an honored ancestor may have evoked fear of his ghost and awe of his earlier achievements (see Figures 2.12 and 2.13). She thus interprets the vase painting depicting male and female figures sharing wine and other offerings with an enormous serpent (see Figures 2.14 and 2.15) as "a couple of healing divinities—hero and heroine divinized" (1991: 348). For Harrison the male gods, whom she viewed as a foreign imposition upon the indigenous population and overlain upon the older heroes' cults, lacked the authenticity she associated with the native, the original, and the chthonic. Perhaps the most important reason for Harrison's "disappointment," however, lies with Harrison herself. For her the male gods, like the male God of her childhood, had no spiritual resonance, whereas the goddesses were real, living spiritual powers, alive for her as

Figure 2.12. Grave mound with serpent, man with a sword is making an oath.

Figure 2.13. Altar to a hero, with serpents and hollow cup for libations.

Figure 2.14. Vase painting showing a man at a banquet, offering a libation to a serpent. On the reverse a goddess receives offerings of oïnochoe, cakes, and lighted taper from a girl.

Figure 2.15. Hero reclining with serpent, woman and boy bringing fruits.

they had been in antiquity. She projected her own spiritual experience onto the historical record of Greek religion: the authentic, living goddesses had been driven underground by inauthentic, imposed male gods.

The gods in Harrison's account, having usurped the cultic observances dedicated to these magnified, heroized dead ancestors, possessed none of the numinosity, the omnipotence, or the grandeur of the goddesses. They did not arise organically from the strong, primitive emotions embodied by the *keres*. None of

the gods had ever been the solitary, all-powerful deity as the local goddess originally was. Even in the Hellenistic and Roman periods they were not merged into a unitary male god-figure as was the goddess Venus Genetrix. As if the gods' usurpation of the hero-cults were not sufficiently disappointing, these male godlings went on to usurp the powers, positions, and cults of the goddesses, their much more powerful predecessors. Harrison takes Zeus and Apollo in particular to task for such patriarchal chauvinism.

Harrison's proposed origin for the gods is not as persuasive as her origin for the goddesses. It is entirely possible that the gods arose much as did the goddesses: some or all of them may have been local, indigenous deities while other deities may have arrived with the incoming Indo-Europeans, alone or as a group pantheon, possibly originally formless, possibly passing through a phase of theriomorphism before finally becoming fully anthropomorphic. The translation of the Linear B tablets since Harrison's death reveals that male gods already existed in the Greek world during its earliest attested stage, the Mycenean Age.[5]

LATER CRITICISM OF HARRISON'S WORK

Whereas there is still agreement that some goddesses, such as Hera at Argos and Mycenae and Athene at Athens were autochthonous, primordial deities of their locales, other goddesses and gods are now thought to be of foreign origin. Artemis and Apollo are believed to have non-Greek origins, having come from Lycia in Asia Minor (Burkert 1985: 144, 149). Aphrodite is yet another goddess neither originally indigenous nor imposed by Indo-European immigrants. Instead, she arrived from the Semitic Near East, where she was the goddess of love Ishtar-Astarte (Burkert 1985: 152–53). The Mycenean Greeks seem to have encountered her when they migrated to Cyprus in the twelfth century BC. Finally, Otto and Kerényi have suggested the intriguing possibility that Dionysus, the god the Greeks themselves characterized as

a foreigner of Thracian or Asiatic origin, may not be foreign at all. Rather, they suggest, he is the god whose very nature is foreignness, "the god who comes" but who is also always already there, who invades from without (Otto 1965: 79; Kerényi 1976: 139–41; Dodds 1957: 270ff).

Since the publication of *Prolegomena*, a larger criticism has emerged regarding Harrison's theories regarding the primacy of the goddesses over the gods, which she adopted from Bachofen's theory of primordial matriarchy. Robert Graves continued the scholarly promotion of primordial matriarchal religion in his *The Greek Myths* (1955) and *The White Goddess* (1948). Beginning in the 1970s, anthropologist Marija Gimbutas produced a series of works in which she interpreted her archeologic findings from Neolithic Southeastern Europe as supporting the existence of a peaceful, matriarchal, Earth goddess based religious system during the Neolithic period. She believed that this matriarchal society was overrun by invading warlike, patriarchal "Kurgan" people, pastoral nomads who brought with them religious systems based on warlike, male sky-gods.[6]

Not surprisingly, this view has come under critical review and is now no longer widely accepted.[7] Most contemporary archeologists and anthropologists reject the idea of a prehistoric matriarchy, although they do recognize the existence of matrilineal societies that may or may not have also been goddess-worshipping societies.[8]

While some of Harrison's proposals about the origins of the goddesses and gods have now come to be questioned, this casts no shadow over the quality of her work. She was developing her theories based on the still rather scant archeological and artistic evidence available to her that has increased vastly since then. Moreover, she was building upon theories, some of which, such as those of Bachofen, are now discredited but were widely accepted at the time. We should not lose sight of her contributions that have withstood the test of time, above all those in the studies of women's cults, rituals, and mysteries in Greek religion.

Finally, we might soften our criticisms of the ideas put forward by Harrison and others of her time when we remember that

much of what we accept as true today regarding Greek religion may be found in the future to be mistaken.

NOTES

1. Between 1870 and 1890 Schliemann (1822–1890) excavated what are believed to be the ruins of Troy near Hissarlik, Turkey. In 1876 he began excavations at Mycenae and in 1884 he worked at the excavation of Tiryns with Wilhelm Dörpfeld, the archeologist with whom Harrison also worked.

   Evans (1851–1941) excavated the city of Knossos on Crete. It was Evans who coined the term "Minoan" for the Bronze Age civilization he discovered there. At Knossos he discovered numerous clay tablets inscribed in Linear A and Linear B.
2. The theories of cultural evolution elaborated by E. B. Tylor (1832–1917) had a great influence on Harrison and on her generation. Tylor believed that a uniform evolutionary sequence of stages was followed in all cultures, at all times. If a culture appeared "savage" to us at present, it was because that "savage" culture either had not yet embarked upon the evolutionary sequence or was still some steps behind European culture.

   For Tylor, a culture's myths represented a primitive attempt at explanation of the physical phenomena of the world, a "primitive counterpart to [modern] science" (Segal *Myth* 14–21). However, "[m]yth is not to be looked on as mere error and folly, but as an interesting product of the human mind. It is sham history, the fictitious narrative of events that never happened" (qtd. in Ackerman *Myth* 39). Tylor created the term "animism" to indicate the tendency of "primitives" and "savages," like children, to see physical aspects of the world as alive, animated. Harrison's adoption of Tylor's "survival" from earlier, savage states of a given society is essential to her understanding of the formation of the older stratum of Greek religion.

   Harrison fills in the lengthy evolutionary gap between primitive animism and fully formed anthropomorphic gods with personalities, departmentalized powers, and stories. She traces in Greek religion the development from non-objectified fears and animated objects, through personified figures that lack names and stories, to theriomorphic deities, to anthropomorphic deities. Yet even in the later anthropomorphic deities, Harrison sees "survivals" of these deities' earlier theriomorphic avatars.

3. Max Müller (1823–1900) was an Indologist, Sanskritist, and translator of the Rig-Veda. His understanding of myth was very influential in the 1860s and 1870s. Müller's theories of myth were heavily dependent on his theories of language. He believed that not only were the languages of Europe and India derived from a common Indo-European (or "Aryan") ancestor, but that their myths were as well.

   According to Müller's idiosyncratic theory early Indo-European ancestor language lacked words for abstraction, having only words for action. Thus:

   > Where we speak the sun following the dawn, the ancient poets could only speak and think of the Sun loving and embracing the Dawn. What is with us a sunset, was to them the Sun growing old, decaying, or dying. Our sunrise was to them the Night giving birth to a beautiful child; and in the Spring they really saw the Sun or the Sky embracing the earth with a warm embrace, and showering treasures into the lap of nature. (Müller "Comparative Mythology" 63–64, qtd. in Ackerman *Myth* 27–28)

   Because he believed that nearly all of these myths were originally solar myths, he and his followers came to be known as "solar mythologists." Moreover, because of the necessarily metaphoric nature of this hypothesized Indo-European language, myths represented a "degradation of meaning," or in Müller's famous phrase "a disease of language" (qtd. in Ackerman 1991a: 28).
4. In her description of the origin of gods Harrison relies upon the ancient theory of Euhemerism (named after one of its early proponents, Euhemerus, early fourth century BC), according to which gods are said to arise by the deification of dead heroes. Harrison draws a sharp contrast between the origins of Greek gods and goddesses. Whereas the gods arise by a combination of Euhemerist deification of dead heroes and the later imposition over them of male sky gods of Iron Age invaders, the goddesses are immeasurably older, having arisen by stages through gradual embodiment of inchoate fears of natural forces.

   Harrison argues that Herakles was a hero caught midway on the transition from hero to god:

   > [Herakles] is allowed the Olympian burnt sacrifice, he is passed through the folds of Hera's robe to make him her child by adoption, he is married in Olympus to Hebe, herself but newly translated, the vase-painter diligently paints his reception into Olympus, he is always elaborately entering, yet he is never really *in*, he is too much a

man to wear at ease the livery of an Olympian, and literature, always over-Olympianized, makes him too often the laughingstock of the stage. (1991: 346–47)

The gods (as well as the goddesses) were often referred to with epithets, a "second name" following the more familiar one. Harrison argues that in some cases such epithets reveal the name of the hero whose cult later was taken over by a god. She gives the example of Zeus Meilichios, suggesting that Meilichios (whose name is itself a euphemism, meaning "gentle, mild, soothing") was originally a hero at whose grave offerings were made (1991: 12–28). She further notes that "Zeus made an attempt to take over the cult of Amphiaraos, as he had taken over the cult of Meilichios; we hear of a Zeus Amphiaraos, but the attempt was not a great success; probably the local hero Amphiaraos, himself all but a god, was too strong for the Olympian" (1991: 28).

5. In the early 1950s, after hearing a lecture by Arthur Evans, Michael Ventris (1922–1956) deciphered Linear B, showing that it was a form of the Greek language. In this he was assisted by John Chadwick (1920–1998), building on the work of Alice Kober (1906–1950). Linear B was the written language of Bronze Age Greece in Mycenae and Pylos and of late Bronze Age Crete (Linear A, which remains undeciphered today, was an even earlier written language employed in Bronze Age Crete). When these Linear B tablets were now read they were found to contain the names of not only of multiple goddesses, but also of gods: Poseidon, Zeus, Dionysos, Enyalios, Paean, and possibly Hermes and Ares (Burkert 1985: 43–44). This evidence refutes the theory (accepted by Harrison and her generation) that Bronze Age Greece had been dominated by goddesses and that the male sky gods of Greece entered only later with the Iron Age invasions. Instead, we now know that gods and goddesses coexisted even in early Bronze Age Greece and in later Minoan Crete.
6. By far the most influential proponent of the theory of primordial matriarchy has been the archeomythologist Marija Gimbutas, author of 1974 *The Gods and Goddesses of Old Europe* (republished in 1982 with the titles reversed as *The Goddesses and Gods of Old Europe*), *The Language of the Goddess* (1989) and *The Civilization of the Goddess* (1991). In these works, she did so much to advance and popularize the narrative that prehistorical societies were matriarchal, peaceful, woman-centered, and goddess-worshipping (Eller 2000: 37–38). Although Gimbutas acknowledged the inferential and intuitive nature of her affirmations, her work has come in for the serious scrutiny.

7. In *The Myth of Matriarchal Prehistory* (2000), Eller presents an argument that contradicts the narrative of prehistoric matriarchy that is still dominant in popular culture even as it has been largely abandoned in academia. She demonstrates that this mythic narrative is of very recent origin, having been first promulgated, as noted, by Bachofen in 1861. Eller does not argue that matriarchy never existed, but that there is simply no proof to support its historical existence. Nor is there evidence for the currently popular belief that patriarchy is a recent phenomenon, having arisen only some 5,000 years ago, replacing a universal matriarchy that had existed for up to the preceding 1.5 to 2 million years (2000: 3, 20). Rather, she argues the archeological and physical evidence is simply insufficient to say definitively whether matriarchy or patriarchy existed at any given time in prehistory.

   The archeological evidence in support of matriarchy has been interpreted in this highly biased manner to support matriarchy ever since Bachofen. This theory was adopted by Harrison, Friedrich Engels, James George Frazer, Robert Graves, and by the depth psychologists Sigmund Freud, Erich Fromm, and Erich Neumann.

   Eller points out that in analyzing prehistoric art the proponents of matriarchy interpreted an almost limitless list of artistic images and motifs as indicative of matriarchy and goddess-worship (2000: 119).

   Harrison's work, beginning with *Prolegomena*, coming as it did only forty-two years after Bachofen's *Mutterrecht*, followed his matriarchal narrative in its discussion of the origin of the goddesses. Eller's revisionary work, which undermines the fundamental narrative underlying Harrison's (and Bachofen's and Frazer's) outline of history, calls into question such theories. The geographical and temporal range covered by Harrison's study was much more limited than that of Gimbutas, since she took into consideration only Greek religion and limited herself to the time from the late Bronze Age to the classical and Hellenistic periods.
8. "Matrilineal" societies refer to kinship systems in which ancestral descent is determined through the maternal line whereas "matriarchy" indicates societal governance by women. Historical and archeological evidence for the former exists but conclusive evidence for the latter is scant to absent.

CHAPTER 3

HARRISON'S RITUAL THEORIES

REVISIONS BASED ON ART AND ARCHEOLOGY, ANTHROPOLOGY, SOCIOLOGY, PSYCHOLOGY, AND EVOLUTION

Harrison is today primarily remembered as a ritualist, a scholar who viewed ritual as prior to myth and, more importantly, as the central member of the group known today as the "Cambridge Ritualists," which also included Gilbert Murray, Francis Cornford, and A. B. Cook. Harrison's major contribution to ritualism[1] began with *Prolegomena to the Study of Greek Religion* in 1903 and reached its peak with the publication of *Themis* in 1912. Along the way, her understanding changed in response to contemporary breakthroughs in the fields of archeology, anthropology, sociology, folklore, psychology, and biological and cultural evolution.

Among the most important influences on Harrison's changing understanding of ritual were the recent advances in comparative and evolutionary anthropology and folklore study. Her relationship with the older generation of classicists was often contentious. Such was her relationship with William Ridgeway, the Disney Professor of Archaeology and a colleague at Newnham College, Cambridge, to which she had returned in 1898 as a Research Fellow and College Lecturer in Classical Archeology. Ridgeway was both a source of ideas for Harrison and an obstruction to her own innovative ideas, especially those influenced by her positive appreciation of current discoveries in the field of evolutionary

anthropology. On the one hand, as Harrison acknowledges in the preface to *Prolegomena,* Ridgeway's claim that the earlier culture of the Mycenaeans of Crete and Greece, the dark-haired people called by Herodotus "Pelasgians," had been overlaid by that of invaders from the north, the later bright-haired Homeric Achaeans, was an important contribution to her own understanding. On the other hand, Ridgeway and his generation more broadly, which had only grudgingly come to accept the recent findings of archeology, now often opposed newer findings coming from fields such as anthropology, whereas Harrison was one of the brash, young classicists attempting to revolutionize the study of Greek religion by incorporating these very new findings.

Harrison was particularly impressed by how Edward Burnett Tylor had transposed Darwin's biological theory of evolution into a theory of cultural evolution; the idea that cultures and their mythologic systems undergo a similar process of evolution. For Tylor, a culture's myths represented its attempt at explanation of the physical phenomena of the world, a "primitive counterpart to [modern] science" (R. Segal 2015: 14–21). However, he also stated that "[m]yth is not to be looked on as mere error and folly, but as an interesting product of the human mind. It is sham history, the fictitious narrative of events that never happened" (qtd. in Ackerman 1991a: 39). Tylor created the term "animism" to indicate the tendency of "primitives" and "savages," like children, to see physical aspects of the world as alive, animated. Harrison's adoption of Tylor's ideas about the "survival" in the later stages of a culture's history of some of its earliest perspectives, is essential to her understanding of the lower, earlier stratum of Greek religion.[2]

In her own work, Harrison sought to fill in the lengthy evolutionary gap between the primitive animism that so fascinated Tylor and the fully formed anthropomorphic gods of classical Greece. She traces the development from non-objectified fears and animated objects, through barely personified figures that lack names and stories, to theriomorphic deities, and then finally to anthropomorphic deities. Yet, even in these later anthropomorphic deities Harrison sees "survivals" of their earlier

theriomorphic avatars. The owl, the olive tree, and the serpent are not merely Athene's attributes: Athene originally *was* the owl, the olive tree, and the serpent. According to Harrison, Homer's epithets for the gods reflect their earlier incarnations. Hera is not merely "ox-eyed," she used to *be* an ox.

WILLIAM ROBERTSTON SMITH

In order to understand Harrison's contributions to the advancement of ritualism, it is important to have at least a cursory understanding of those scholars on whose work she built; scholars whose influence she was always ready to acknowledge.

William Robertson Smith (1846–1894) was arguably the most important of these intellectual forebears. Smith, a Biblical scholar, a theologian, and a student of Semitic religions, was among the first to assert that religion was a matter of "things done," rather than of things believed or experienced.

> Smith was the first to see the era of primitive ... religion as practice rather than belief—as ritual than either creed or myth. Myth for Smith arises to account above all for the ritual of the annual killing of the totem, or god. (R. Segal 1991: viii)

Smith was a "ritualist" *avant le nom.* Most importantly, Smith was "the first scholar who tried to formulate the relationship between myth and ritual in terms of what should be considered as primary and what as secondary" (Bošković 2021: 77). He was very clear in seeing that ritual is primary and myth only a secondary attempt at explanation of ritual, often after a ritual's purpose and function has been forgotten. He argued that myth was not invented to explain ritual that was misunderstood but rather to explain ritual that was no longer understood but still practiced.[3] Smith states that:

> [I]n almost every case the myth was derived from the ritual, and not the ritual from the myth ... the myth is merely

> the explanation of a religious usage; and ordinarily it is such an explanation as could not have arisen till the original sense of the usage had more or less fallen into oblivion. (Smith "Lectures on the Religion of the Semites" 19, qtd. in R. Segal 1998b: 2)

Because he believed myth to be "merely the explanation" of ritual, Smith further believed that the study of myth was of secondary importance to that of ritual:

> It follows that mythology ought not to take the prominent place that is too often assigned to it in the scientific study of ancient faiths. So far as the myths consist of explanation of ritual, their value is altogether secondary, and it may be affirmed with confidence that in almost every case the myth was derived from the ritual and not the ritual from the myth; for the ritual was fixed and the myth was variable, the ritual was obligatory and faith in the myth was at the discretion of the worshipper ... [I]n the study of ancient religions we must begin, not with myth, but with ritual and traditional usage. (Smith 1894: 17–18)

The principal social ritual studied by Smith was animal sacrifice. According to his analysis the sacrificial animal was a totem-animal, an animal whose killing was normally taboo, but which was killed on certain religious occasions and entirely consumed by a totemic brethren. As Robert Segal has shown:

> Smith is rightly viewed as a pioneering sociologist of religion. He shifts focus of the study of primitive and ancient religion from beliefs to institutions and from the individual to the group. For Smith, the function of primitive and ancient religion is the preservation of the group, even if he does not, like the more relentlessly sociological Durkheim, make group experience the origin of religion or make the group itself the object of worship. (qtd. in Bošković 2021: 108)

Harrison's earlier understanding of ritual, especially the view put forward in *Prolegomena,* built directly upon the work of Smith, while her later ideas expressed in *Themis* and *Ancient Art and Ritual* (1913), as we will see, move in a sharply different direction.

JAMES GEORGE FRAZER

It would be difficult to overstate the impact that Frazer's *The Golden Bough* (1922) had upon the intellectual world of the late nineteenth and early twentieth centuries. Harrison and the other "Cambridge Ritualists" relied heavily on his work, at least at first, particularly the ideas central to *The Golden Bough* about the dying god and the "tragic rhythm" of death and resurrection.

Frazer carried forward the approach of comparative evolutionary anthropology pioneered by E. B. Tylor and by William Robertson Smith.

> From Smith, Frazer took both the association of myth with ritual and the ritual of killing the god. He altered the exact connection between the myth and the ritual, made the god the god of vegetation, and made the function of the ritual agricultural: causing the crops to grow. Frazer also introduced the role of the king, the incarnation of the god of vegetation. Where Smith restricts himself to Semitic cultures, Frazer boldly generalizes to primitive and ancient ones worldwide. Strictly speaking, myth-ritualism for Frazer arises neither in his stage of magic nor even in his stage of religion but only in a subsequent, less clearly demarcated stage of magic and religion combined—the stage to which nearly all of the *The Golden Bough* is devoted. (R. Segal 1991: viii)

Frazer considered himself deeply indebted to his close friend Smith, but his view of the relation between myth and ritual is

sharply different. Where Smith saw rituals as primary and earlier, and as originally and essentially independent of myths that were only subsequently attached to them, Frazer saw myth as primary, with ritual occurring later as an "acting out" of the myth.

> In Frazer's true myth-ritualist scenario, myth arises prior to ritual rather than, as for Smith, after it. The myth that gets enacted in the combined stage emerges in the stage of religion and therefore antedates the ritual to which it is applied. In the combined stage, myth, as for Smith, explains the point of ritual, but not only once the meaning of ritual has been forgotten. Rather, myth *gives* ritual its meaning. In the combined stage, ritual would not be undertaken without myth: one would not ritualistically enact the death and rebirth of that god. (Segal 1998b: 5)

Frazer extended the ethnological approach pioneered by Wilhelm Mannhardt in his study of contemporary central European peasant customs into the realm of Greco-Roman antiquity. Frazer identified three stages of cultural evolution, beginning with magic and progressing through religion to science. But whereas Frazer used the methods of cultural anthropology and comparative mythology to evaluate the evolution of the fertility and vegetation myths of Northern and Central Europe and the Mediterranean basin as they progressed toward Christianity (and ultimately beyond Christianity to philosophy and science), Harrison was more interested in how Greek religion evolved from one dominated by subterranean fertility deities and the placation of ancestral spirits, *daimones*, and malign spirits such as *keres*, into the religion of the Olympian gods.

From Frazer, Harrison took up the important concept of the vegetation myth and the motifs of the *hieros gamos* (sacred wedding) and the dying and reborn god. She took up from Tylor, Smith, and Frazer the evolutionary approach of comparative anthropology and applied it to Greek religion. However, Harrison went on to challenge Frazer's concept of cultural

evolution as she applied it to Greek religion and mythology. Moreover, she did not take up Frazer's linear schema of evolution from magic to religion to science.

NIETZSCHE

Finally, brief mention must be made of how important Nietzsche's *Birth of Tragedy* (1872) was to the Cambridge Ritualists;[4] especially his suggestion that a Dionysian religion preceded the sunny Olympian religion of Greek art and myth, which overlaid and obscured it. The parallels with Harrison's views about the two strata of Greek religion, chthonic and Olympian, are unmistakable. Like Nietzsche, she was suspicious of the bright, rational surface of Greek culture popularized by the nineteenth-century Romantic movement.

For Nietzsche, the submerged, irrational element of Greek religion is embodied in what he terms the "Dionysian" element:

> It is an uncontested tradition that Greek tragedy in its oldest form dealt only with the sufferings of Dionysus, and that for a long time Dionysus was the only theatrical hero. But we may claim with equal certainty that, until Euripides, Dionysus never ceased to be the tragic hero, and that all the celebrated characters of the Greek stage—Prometheus, Oedipus and so on—are merely masks of that original hero, Dionysus. (Nietzsche 1993: 51)

Nietzsche claims the later developments of fifth-century theater all grew out of the primordial, submerged "Dionysian" element of Greek religion; that all fifth-century Greek tragedy, most of whose plots were derived from Homeric epics and often involved Olympian gods, overlay the bones of the ancient Dionysian stratum. Harrison's grand theme in *Prolegomena* of the rediscovery of the ancient stratum of irrational, chthonic religion underlying the later, more rational Olympian religion mirrors Nietzsche's assertion of the ancient, irrational "Dionysian" stratum underlying

the entire culture of classical Athens, especially the tragedies of Euripides and the philosophies of Socrates and Plato.

Harrison took from Nietzsche a deep suspicion, not only of the Olympian gods but of all surface phenomena. Her work, especially in *Prolegomena,* is characterized by a search for the religion that had been submerged and concealed.

HARRISON'S REVISION OF RITUALS AND FESTIVALS

Harrison follows Frazer in seeing magic—the most primitive form of technology—as part of the earliest phase of spiritual development. In *The Golden Bough,* Frazer describes the magic of primitives as having both positive and negative aspects. Positive, inductive magic is a creative activity designed to provide for the primary needs of humankind: food, rain, and fertility. Negative, apotropaic magic exists to avert malign influences. Harrison departs from Frazer in seeing early magic as primarily negative, as a technology of aversion (*apotrope*), placation, and riddance of malign physical forces, and only very secondarily as inducing fertility. While Harrison recognizes the importance to primitives of magic as a means of obtaining what they needed, in *Prolegomena* she gives far greater emphasis to magical attempts to avert things feared: death, disease, and dead ancestors. In her discussions of the women's festivals and harvest festivals, Harrison begins with Frazer's schema of the evolution from magic through religion to philosophy (understanding philosophy to include what we would term science, technology based on rational cognition). She adopts Frazer's definition of magic as the manipulation of the physical world in order to force changes in it; that is, as a primitive form of technology. However, she quickly veers away from his active, positive definition of magic to focus on primitive attempts to avert spiritual energies rather than to evoke them. Moreover, while she begins with Frazer's linear schema of evolution from magic to religion to philosophy, she does not stay with it, instead seeing only the evolution from magic to religion.

CHTHONIC AND OLYMPIAN RELIGIONS

Perhaps the central contention of Harrison's *Prolegomena* was the distinction of the early stage of Greek religion, that of the chthonic deities, the *keres*, and the Goddess, from the later religion of the Olympian gods that appeared to replace it. Her approach, influenced by the study of art and anthropology, emphasized the radical difference between the rituals dedicated to the Olympian gods from those offered to the earlier chthonic deities.

The chthonic cult is immeasurably older, primordial, and had an entirely different feel, different rituals, and different language. This form of religion lacked temples, altars, and sculpted images (but did, apparently, have a few painted images). There were no processions. Instead, it focussed on fasting, cleansing, purgation, and atonement. As a cult of the Earth and the Underworld, it had a dark, gloomy, chilly atmosphere: "Styx is the chill cold water of death, Hades and the Erinyes are 'chilly ones' (στυγεροί) [stugeroi], the epithet is utterly aloof from Zeus" (Harrison 1991: 15). Its purpose was the placation and aversion (*apotrope*), the sending away (*apopompe*) of the Underworld beings: Ge/Gaia (Earth), heroes, dead ancestors, ghosts, and *keres* (malignant spirits). The people engaged in these rites to placate these beings and to make them go away and leave them in peace: *do ut abeas* [I give so that you should leave]. Harrison's invention of the phrase *do ut abeas* is in conscious distinction to the more familiar phrase *do ut des* [I give so that you [the god] should give]. She thus underlines again, and in a new way, the distinction between the Olympian and chthonic deities and their associated rituals: sacrificial rituals are "given" to the Olympian gods so that they might in turn give to the givers, but rituals are given to the chthonic gods only so that they might go away and stay away.

In the chthonic rituals, the sacrificed animals were black, the rituals occurred at sundown or at night, and were performed facing the setting sun in the west. The sacrificed animal had its head held downward at the time of sacrifice so that it was facing the

Underworld. These sacrifices were not shared by the people; they were not feasts. Instead, they were "devoted" in their entirety to the Underworld by being burned in their entirety. The language of this religion is distinct from that used for the Olympians. The words for these chthonic forms of sacrifice are distinct: *sphazein* [to slay or slaughter the sacrifice by slitting the throat], *enagizein* [to offer a sacrifice to the dead], and *holokautein* [to burn entirely; hence the English word "holocaust"], (1991: 55). Another term closely associated with the older, chthonic cult is *deisidaimonia* ["fear of spirits"]. This term was used pejoratively by writers of the later classical period to denigrate the popular religion as "superstition" and to urge that this form of "superstition" should be left behind by rulers and the better sort of people (1991: 4–7).

In contrast, the religion of the Olympian gods was characterized by the term *therapeia* ("tendance"), a word that has the general sense of giving service to and "taking care" of the gods. It was for these gods that the temples and altars were built, and the magnificent anthropomorphic images sculpted. The rituals dedicated to them consisted of prayers, processions, games and contests (*agones*), as well as sacrifices of animal offerings that, importantly, were shared with the human celebrants. While one part of the sacrificed animal's body was burned and thus given to the god, the remainder was eaten by the community; the sacrifice was thus a feast shared between the community and the god. This form of sacrifice was termed *thusia* [offering/ sacrifice] and the sacrificial animal a *hiereion* [victim, animal for sacrifice].

The sacrifices to the Olympian gods were conducted at sunrise or in the daytime, with participants facing the rising sun at the east side of the temple and were characterized by a joyful atmosphere of feasting. The animals sacrificed were usually white in color (1991: 64) and their heads were held back at the time of sacrifice so that they were facing upwards, toward the Olympian gods. The celebrants likewise raised their hands upwards toward the Ouranian ("heavenly") gods. The smoke from the burning animal's flesh was believed to be a smell pleasing to the gods (a belief echoed in Hinduism and in the Hebrew scriptures).

Early in *Prolegomena* Harrison examined the Diasia festival; one nominally dedicated to Zeus but in which she discovers "survivals" of the earlier religion, evidence of the persistence of the earlier chthonic religion. Following this, at the heart of the book are three chapters dedicated to the Anthesteria festival, the harvest festivals (including the Thargelia), and women's festivals (including the Thesmophoria). In her dissection of these festivals, she shows how those nominally dedicated to an Olympian deity had their roots in rituals dedicated to chthonic deities. The names of these four festivals did not refer to the Olympian gods to which they were ostensibly dedicated, and their rituals were not characterized by the *therapeia* (tendance), characteristic of Olympian religion, but rather, by the *apotrope* (aversion), characteristic of the ancient, chthonic religious system.

> In the Anthesteria the ceremonies known as ἐναγισμοί [enagismoi] were seen to be purifications (καθαρμοί) [katharmoi], and by purifications were meant placations of Keres, of ghosts and spirits. In the Thargelia the ceremony of the *pharmakos* was seen to be also a purification, but in the sense not of the placation or riddance of ghosts and sprites but of a magical cleansing from physical evil. In the Thesmophoria the ceremony with the pigs was preceded by ceremonies of purification, and was in itself of magical intent. (1991: 161)

In each of these chapters, Harrison follows the pattern she set down in her chapter on the Diasia, revealing through the examination of art and ritual how these festivals were of incalculable age, and how they were originally dedicated to older deities (often goddesses), and how they had come to be overlain by dedication to later, Olympian deities. By looking briefly at Harrison's interpretation of each of these festivals we can see how she relies not only on textual information, but also on the evidence found in vase paintings and other artworks, and on the newer techniques of comparative anthropology.

DIASIA

In fifth-century Athens the Diasia was a festival dedicated to the Olympian god Zeus, under his name of Zeus Meilichios. It was carried out at night and involved libations (wine poured out onto the ground, into trenches) and holocaust sacrifices. The skins of the sacrificed animals, which were believed to have purifying properties, were kept to be used in subsequent processions. Harrison's suspicion that this festival was not originally dedicated to Zeus was aroused when she learned that (according to the Scholiast on Lucian) these rites were accompanied by a "chilly gloom," a feature that seemed to her inconsistent with a festival dedicated to an Olympian deity. This led her to examine bas reliefs found in the harbor at Peireus, a place known to be associated with the worship of Zeus Meilichios. She found that one of the reliefs, which was inscribed with a dedication to Zeus Meilichios, depicted the god in the form of a serpent. The serpent was not a form in which Olympian Zeus was ever depicted but rather one often used to represent an Underworld deity. Further, the fact that the rites were conducted at night, rather than at dawn or daytime, the holocaust nature of the sacrifice, and that libations were poured out in trenches in the Earth, all seemed to her to suggest that this rite had originally been dedicated to a chthonic deity of the dead addressed by the euphemistic name of Meilichios (meaning mild, gentle, gracious or kind) (1991: 12–22).

Harrison noted that in the Athenian calendar the months of the year were named not for any of the Olympian deities, but rather for ancient rituals that long predated worship of the Olympians (1991: 30). For instance, the month in which the Diasia was celebrated was called Maimakterion, which suggests that "Meilichios" was in some sense also "Maimaktes," meaning "he who rages eager, panting and thirsting for blood" (1991: 17). She thus concluded that beneath the veneer of a festival dedicated to the Olympian god Zeus, fifth-century Athenians were still faithfully carrying out a ritual that was clearly originally performed for the purpose of placation of dead ancestors, and

originally dedicated to the chthonic *daemon*, Maimaktes, but which was now dedicated to the Olympian deity, Zeus, as Zeus Meilichios.

Harrison sees the literary myths about the punishment in Hades of figures such as Salmoneus, Tityos, Tantalos, Sisyphos, and the Danaides for offenses against the Olympian gods as being late revisions. Originally these figures were not mortals undergoing Underworld punishment but rather the older Underworld divinities, the *daimones* of the Old Order. These new myths represent the displacement of the *daimones* by the later Olympian deities (1991: 335–36, 606–9, 613–22). What makes them offensive to the later-arriving Olympian gods is not hubris but rather simply their pre-existence and their continuing existence, submerged but still powerful. Indeed, Harrison came to believe that these older, Underworld *daimones* and gods continued to be worshipped even into late antiquity (and possibly well into the Middle Ages) with sacrifices very different from those given to the Olympian gods.

ANTHESTERIA

The Anthesteria, which gave its name to the month of Anthesterion, was in fifth-century Athens dedicated to Dionysus, but Harrison showed it to be originally a ritual focussed on placating the spirits of the dead and chthonic *daimones*, a daemonic "All Souls' Day." This three-day ritual was celebrated in late winter/early spring (February/March in our calendar) and involved general drunkenness and revelry.

On the first day, Pithoigia, the casks of the previous autumn's vintage were opened and drunk as a first-fruits offering. On the second day, *Choes*, the drinking continued and a *hieros gamos* (sacred wedding) was celebrated, in which Dionysus was married to the wife of the King Archon (1991: 33), a sacred marriage that recalled Dionysos's marriage to Ariadne, who had been abandoned by Theseus, as well as to Erigone, the daughter of Ikarios who had been taught the art of viticulture by

Dionysos. The sacred marriage took place in the Boukolion, the "ox-herd's house" in the Agora. We do not know with certainty what took place during the night of the ritual marriage, whether the King Archon's wife slept with an image of Dionysos, with the King Archon himself in disguise, or with another person (Burkert 1985: 238–40). This sacred marriage between the god and the King Archon's wife suggests a marriage of god with *polis*. Libations were poured and, as might be expected, a loosening of social mores and a general carnival atmosphere obtained.

On the third day, a porridge of mixed grains and beans was prepared in individual pots. This pottage was associated with the myth of the Flood of Deucalion, according to which the people found only these items to eat after the flood.

Harrison finds numerous strikingly unusual aspects to these festival days. The second and third days of the festival, the *Choes* and *Chytroi*, were observed with apotropaic precautions. On these days the people chewed buckthorn (a purgative) and painted their doors with pitch, ritual forms of apotropaism directed against the spirits of the dead.

Despite the wine-drinking and the carnival atmosphere, all three days of the festival were, perhaps paradoxically, characterized by a general air of gloom. This was attributed by the Athenians to a number of myths: the killing and dismemberment of Dionysos, Orestes' defilement by his matricide, the killing of Ikarios, the suicide by hanging of Ikarios' daughter Erigone, as well as a myth regarding the killing of Aetolians who brought wine to Athens and were killed there. These myths of killing and blood-shedding are related to wine-making; the wine from the grape is the blood of the god Dionysos (Burkert 1985: 238). Harrison's purpose in relating the connection of these myths to the rituals of Anthesteria is to show they are all examples of etiologic myths; that is, myths created to explain rituals "misunderstood." She demonstrates inconsistencies in the connections between these myths with the practices of the rituals, how the myths were not truly connected with their rituals. She shows

instead that the rituals originated as a means for the aversion (*apotrope*) of *keres* and the ghosts of dead ancestors.

Much of the evidence Harrison adduces to explain the origin of the Anthesteria as a collection of apotropaic rites and to counter its associated etiologic myths comes from her close examination of art. As we have already noted, she was a pioneer in the use of art as evidence in the reassessment of the origins of Greek religion.

She demonstrates this with an analysis of a vase painting that shows Hermes Psychopompos evoking the dead, commanding them up and out of the earth (Figure 3.1).

In his left hand, Hermes holds the *kerykeion* (*caduceus,* herald's staff) that identifies him as Hermes Psychopompos (Hermes, leader of the dead to the Underworld). But Harrison points out a small detail that is easily missed: in his left hand, Hermes carries a rod (*rhabdos*). The function of the *rhabdos* is to "sway others," to command. Circe used such a *rhabdos* to transform Odysseus' men into swine (Harrison 1991: 44). In this painting, the *rhabdos* of Hermes Psychopompos is the magic wand he uses to command and lead the dead out from the cask:

> This magic wand became the attribute of all who hold sway over the dead. It is the wand, not the scepter, that is the token of life or death ... The rhabdos as magic wand was πεισίβροτος, *enchanter* of the dead, before it became as sceptre πεισίβροτος, *ruler* of mortals. (1991: 45)

The huge casks had multiple uses and could be used both for wine-storage and for burial of the dead. While Harrison does not claim to prove that the cask in this vase painting is part of the Anthesteria, she employs it to provide a plausible reason for the "gloomy atmosphere" of Anthesteria: that the original focus of the Anthesteria rituals was not the opening of wine-casks as part of a celebration of new wine, but rather on the releasing of the spirits of the dead from huge burial casks by Hermes Psychopompos. The myths of Dionysos as wine god and of other the figures

Figure 3.1. Hermes Psychopompos, with caduceus and rhabdos, evoking spirits of the dead from a burial pithos.

associated with wine-making (Ikarios, Erigone, Orestes, and the Aetolians) were late additions, created to explain a ritual after its original function had been forgotten, a "ritual misunderstood."

Harrison regards the timing of this ritual as significant, since late winter/early spring was believed to be the time when the dead were thought to awaken and rise, at the same time that the vegetation awakened and began to arise from the Earth. She also suggested, perhaps less convincingly, that the name "Anthesterion" was derived not from *anthos* (flower), but from *ana* (up or back) and *thessasthai* (to pray), that is to revoke, or to "pray back up" the spirits of the dead.

In Harrison's view, just as the Pithoigia was originally a ritual involving the opening of funerary casks rather than wine-casks, the *choes* or cups were originally not used for drinking, but for libations offered to the chthonic *daimones* and the spirits of the dead, and the *chytroi* were not originally pots, but naturally occurring clefts in the Earth into which the dead were buried. That on the third day of Anthesteria (*Chytroi*) a dish of cooked seeds was offered not to any of the Olympian deities, but to Hermes Chthonios, was in her view a further indication that this ritual was not originally dedicated to the Olympian god Dionysus, but to Underworld deities and spirits (*Chthonios*). Moreover, the fact that the food offering was not shared by the human participants, indicates its chthonian nature.

Harrison brings into her discussion a Greek proverb: "Out of the doors! ye Keres; it is no longer Anthesteria" (1991: 35) and asks: if Anthesteria were only a Dionysian festival of new wine and flowers, how can we explain this proverb? Why the invocation of the Keres in a festival dedicated to Dionysus?

Harrison arrived at her new understanding of Anthesteria not only through close examination of artistic evidence, but also through comparison with literary accounts of the Roman festivals Lemuria (1991: 36), Lupercalia, and Feralia (1991: 51–52). She adduces findings from contemporary comparative anthropology by comparing the Anthesteria to rituals in contemporary Brittany (1991: 33), among "Slavonic" peoples and in India (1991: 36), as well as to contemporary Christian rituals (1991: passim).

THARGELIA

Harrison then turned to the harvest festivals of ancient Greece, principally the Thargelia, again comparing them to similar rituals in ancient Rome and to those of the Arunta people of central Australia described by Andrew Lang. She concluded that the Thargelia too, was rooted in rituals dedicated to the chthonic deities, whose purpose was purification and purgation. However unlike the Anthesteria, in which one was purged of fears associated with ghosts of the dead rising with the spring, the purgation of the Thargelia was from taboo "upon the harvest fruits till all are ripe" (1991: 83). This taboo had to be removed before plant foods such as barley and wheat could be harvested and eaten. By the classical age the Thargelia, which was originally a grain harvest festival, had come to be dedicated to Apollo and Artemis. Harrison showed that the four principal offerings made at the Thargelia were all associated with a far earlier period. These included the *eiresione,* an olive branch wound with wool and hung with grains and fruits, the *nephalia,* a libation of water, honey, milk, and olive oil, the *pelanos,* and the *pharmakon.* The *pelanos* was a pot of barley grains, a primitive form of food no longer eaten by the people but only offered in rituals. Yeast-leavened bread and wine, both fermented foods reflecting later cultural developments, were conspicuously absent.

The ritual of the *pharmakon,* which involved two persons being driven out of the city and flogged, was a very important part of the Thargelia at Athens. The *pharmakoi* were scapegoats, functioning as *katharmoi* ("off-scourings"), whose removal from the city also freed it of evils such as plagues and famines. Harrison makes the surprising and controversial claim that these *pharmakoi* were then killed, that they were human sacrifices. She supports this claim with numerous citations from classical Greek authors. Moreover, she adduces comparisons from Roman rituals and Frazer's collection of similar scapegoating rituals in non-European cultures.

Harrison goes on to discuss the Kallynteria ("sweeping-out festival") and the Plynteria ("washing festival"), as also originally existing for the purpose of purification and cleansing in preparation for the incoming of the first-fruits, not as occasions for giving thanks to or requesting intercession from an Olympian deity such as Apollo or Athene.

THESMOPHORIA

Harrison then turns with even greater interest to her reinterpretation of the women's festivals, focussing principally on the Thesmophoria, with somewhat less attention to the Arrephoria, Skirophoria, Stenia, and Haloa, which she regards as similar in function and form. She believes these festivals were all of "immemorial antiquity," even more primitive than the Anthesteria and Thargelia, and that because of the "mixed contempt and superstition of men ... they were preserved in pristine purity" (1991: 120). These festivals are of great interest to Harrison because she claims that "[u]nlike the Diasia, Antheseria, Thargelia, they were left almost uncontaminated by Olympian usage" (1991: 120). These festivals were mysteries—that is, participants were sworn to secrecy—and thus many of the details of their rituals are only partially known to us. Harrison goes on to make the further claim about these women's festivals, "under the influence of a new religious impulse, they issued at last in the most widely influential of all Greek ceremonials, the Eleusinian Mysteries" (1991: 120). The "new religious impulse" Harrison refers to here is the later importation of Dionysian elements into the ancient women's mystery cults.

In her discussion of the Thesmophoria, as with her evaluations of Diasia, Anthesteria, and harvest festivals, Harrison relies primarily on textual evidence supplemented with her unique use of artistic works. She also turns to comparative anthropology, comparing these women's rituals not only to those of the Romans of antiquity, but to those of various contemporary cultures described by Lang and Frazer.

The Thesmophoria was a three-day women's festival. The first day involved the carrying down (*kathodos*) into underground (chthonic) chambers, known as *megara*, a sacrificed pig, as well as a fir cone (a fertility symbol), and flour-paste figures of serpents and humans, and the carrying up (*anodos*) of the remains of pigs sacrificed the year before. These remains were then used as a kind of fertility charm, an implement of sympathetic magic, in the planting of the new crops. Later, in the classical period, these rituals were understood as a dramatic acting out of an episode in the myth of Persephone and Demeter; the sacrificed pig representing the pigs that fell into the earth with Persephone when she was abducted by Hades. However, Harrison argues persuasively that the ritual was originally an enactment of sympathetic magic, with no goddesses or gods involved at all. Relying on comparative anthropologic data borrowed from Lang and Frazer, she suggests that the pig sacrifice of the Greeks may originally have been a human sacrifice (1991: 125). She is convinced that the myth was a late addition, designed to provide an etiologic explanation for a ritual that was no longer understood when the Greeks ceased to believe in sympathetic magic:

> The myth of the rape of Persephone of course really arose from the ritual, not the ritual from the myth ... the content of the ritual was 'physical,' the object the impulsion of nature ... The festival, he says, is a 'thank-offering' to Demeter. But in the sympathetic magic of the Thesmophoria man attempts direct compulsion, he admits no mediator between himself and nature, and he thanks no god for what no god has done. A thank-offering is later even than a prayer, and prayer as yet is not. To mark the transition from rites of compulsion to rites of supplication and consequent thanksgiving is to read the whole religious history of primitive man. (1991: 124)

The dedication of the Thesmophoria to Demeter Thesmophoros is thus an an instantiation of Harrison's thesis of ritualism: "*ritual practice misunderstood* explains the elaboration of myth" (Verrall 1890: iii).

Harrison subsumes her discussion of the Eleusinian Mysteries under that of the women's festivals and harvest festivals because in her view, these Mysteries originated as one of them: "... at the mysteries there was an offering of first-fruits; the mysteries were in fact the *Thargelia* of Eleusis" (1991: 155). By the classical era, when belief in the Olympian gods had begun to wane, at least among the more sophisticated Greeks, the mystery religions came to be the locus for the expression of profound religious feelings. Harrison proposed that what began as primitive first-fruits rituals obtained much of their religious significance and their connection to the hope of immortality from the influx of Dionysian and Orphic religion: "To Athens the mysteries owe their external magnificence, to Dionysos and Orpheus their deep inward content" (1991: 150).

Harrison puts forward the controversial but intriguing conjecture that the word "mystery" arises not, as is usually thought, from *muo* ("to close," as in closing one's eyes or mouth for the purpose of secrecy), but to *musos* ("pollution"). For her, a mystery is "a rite in which certain sacra are exhibited, which cannot be safely seen by the worshipper till he has undergone certain purifications" (1991: 151). She believes that a central part of the mysteries involved ritual purification from pollution, *musos*. This purification occurred in the early days of the ten-day festival, which included the *elasis* (a "driving out") to the sea, bathing in the sea, fasting, and sacrifice of a pig. This extensive purification was essential before the *mystes* ("initiate") could partake in the central actions of the mysteries: the drinking of the *kykeon* [a potion of water, barley, herbs, and possibly other substances] and the handling of the sacred objects, the *sacra*. Harrison asserts that although we cannot know what precisely the *sacra* consisted of, their handling in the Eleusinian Mysteries was in essence identical to that in the Thesmophoria, the Skirophoria, the Arrephoria and the Haloa, and so may have included "cakes shaped like the symbols of sex" (1991: 149).

Harrison claims that the Eleusinian rituals were not originally dedicated to Demeter or Persephone or indeed to any god or goddess. Rather, their original purpose was "purification as preliminary to the handling of magical sacra and to the partaking of first-fruits" (1991: 162). That is, they originated as rituals of sympathetic fertility magic and became connected to the myth of the rape of Persephone and Demeter's search for her lost daughter only in the classical period.

HARRISON MOVES TOWARD A REVISION OF RITUALISM

After the publication of *Prolegomena* in 1903, Harrison's work shifted direction in response to her reading of Émile Durkheim, Sigmund Freud, Arnold van Gennep, and Henri Bergson, in whose works she found support for the idea of a social, communal origin of religion.

Émile Durkheim

Like Harrison, Durkheim built on the writings of William Robertson Smith, from whom he "took several leading ideas: that primitive religion was a clan cult and that the cult was totemic, that the god was the clan itself divinized, and that totemism was the most elementary or primitive, and in that sense original, form of religion known to us" (Ackerman 1991a: 102). Also from Smith, he took up the idea that "the importance of myths was based on their role in the society" (Bošković 2021: 60). Although Durkheim was already putting forward most of these ideas as early as 1898, they were not immediately known to Harrison or the other Cambridge Ritualists, as his great work *The Elementary Forms of the Religious Life* was published in France in 1912, after the Cambridge Ritualists had published their own most important works between 1908 and 1911. Nevertheless, Harrison and the others were clearly already familiar with his major ideas.[5]

When Harrison highlighted the social origins of religion in *Themis*, she seemed to be abandoning her conviction that the placation of chthonic deities is the central theme of Greek religion and mythology. While it is impossible to know with certainty why Harrison made this shift, between *Prolegomena* and *Themis*, one can look at *Prolegomena* as a working-through of some of Harrison's own psychological issues. The storyline that runs through *Prolegomena* is that dark, barely repressed, underground feminine forces were later suppressed by male deities lounging carefree on Olympus. This can be seen as mirroring the situations Harrison found herself in as she struggled first for an education, then for academic recognition, and finally for a position at the university. She may well have felt herself to be an underground feminine force suppressed by the privileged dons of Cambridge. After publishing *Prolegomena*, she may have felt that her achievements had been well-enough recognized that she could now ease up on the need to strive against the forces of repression. She had been in her fifties when *Prolegomena* appeared and was in her sixties by the time *Themis* was published. She now had a circle of admirers and followers and was no longer an isolated, under-recognized, "underground" intellectual striving against the hard, prejudiced world of male academics. She was now the center of a small group with its own "spirit," the "Cambridge Ritualists," and had her own circles of friends at Cambridge and Oxford. It is, however, important not to view these possible personal aspects as grounds for dismissing the validity of Harrison's claims made in *Prolegomena*.

The differences between *Prolegomena* and *Themis* are stunning. To give but one example, the Anthesteria festival is understood in *Prolegomena* to be directed toward the placation of ancestral ghosts that were rising from the earth in the early spring alongside the re-awakening of the earth and vegetation. However, in *Themis* Harrison discarded this earlier theory and replaced it with the idea that the Anthesteria was simply an early spring fertility festival. She has banished the dead ancestors, the ghosts and "bogeys," the *daemones* and *keres*, and replaced them with a spring fertility rite that binds the participants together.

Harrison now saw the rationalistic view of religion promulgated by Frazer as "explaining away" rather than explaining religion, whereas the Durkheimian view of religion as the projection of the needs and wishes of a social group mirrored her own emerging intuitive sense:

> [religion] is not the aspiration of the individual soul after a god, or after the unknown, or after the infinite; rather it is the expression, utterance, projection of the emotion, the desire of a group ... Religion, in its rise, is indistinguishable from social custom, embodying social emotion. (Harrison 2018: 50, 51)

Sigmund Freud

Harrison began to read Freud's work in the period after completing *Prolegomena* and before beginning *Themis*. She claimed Freud's writings, especially his *Totem and Taboo* (1950), as major influences on her thinking, but it seems that rather than being influenced by them, she instead recognized the congruence of his ideas with her own in their respective fields. Clearly, *Totem and Taboo* could not have influenced *Themis* directly since it was published the year after *Themis*'s publication. Harrison was perhaps too generous in attributing to Freud ideas that were her own and that she later recognized as reflected in his writings.[6] For instance, Freud's psychological theory of "suppression" of the unconscious mirrors Harrison's outline in *Prolegomena* of the "suppression" of the earlier, chthonic religion of Greece by the supervening Olympian religion, and the "return of the suppressed" in the mystery cults with their revitalization of elements of the chthonic religion in the classical period.

Throughout *Themis* and also in *Ancient Art and Ritual*, Harrison consistently introduced ideas that we associate with Freudian psychology to describe the evolution of art (*drama*) from ritual (*dithyramb*). She described this process without ever actually using the term "sublimation," but it seems clear that this is what she meant:

> Psychologists tell us that representations, ideas, imaginations, all the intellectual, conceptual factors in our life

> are mainly due to deferred reactions. If an impulse finds instantly its appropriate satisfaction, there is no representation. It is out of the delay, just the space between the impulse and the reaction, that all our mental life, our images, ideas, our consciousness, our will, most of all our religion, arise. If we were utterly, instantly satisfied, if we were a mass of well contrived instincts, we should have no representation, no memory, no μίμησις [mimesis], no δρώμενα [dromena], no drama. Art and religion alike spring from unsatisfied desire. (1974: 44)

Harrison's thought seems to run parallel to Freud's, rather than borrowing from him (Harrison cites one Dr. P. Beck in relation to the above quote. Indeed, Freud appears nowhere in the Index of *Themis*.) Harrison attributed the origins of art and religion "though perhaps not wholly ritual" to "unsatisfied desire" and "deferred reactions" (2007: 21), years before Freud proposed that civilization itself and all of its creations arise as the necessary sublimation of aggressive impulses.

At some points in *Themis* Harrison employed near-Freudian terminology, as in her use of the term "subconscious," rather than Freud's "unconscious": "It might almost be said that the Olympians stand for articulate consciousness, the Eniautos-Daimon of the subconscious" (1974: xxi).

Along with Harrison and most thinkers of the nineteenth and early twentieth centuries, Freud accepted the theory of primordial matriarchy (Freud 1950: 179; 1967: 104–6, 168–69) and that goddesses preceded gods.[7] However, unlike Harrison Freud always moved quickly to discussion of father gods. In his project of demystifying religion, pathologizing it as a societal, cultural neurosis, he smashed the idols of gods but not those of the goddesses (Freud 1961: 38).

While for Harrison the goddess was the predominant concern, for Freud the mother was most important.[8] For both Harrison and Freud, the feminine (goddess and mother) exhibited aspects of death.[9]

Although both Harrison and Freud shared the skepticism of the nineteenth century's intellectuals toward Christianity, they incorporated this skepticism into their work in diverging ways. Freud saw religion as a cultural neurosis, a "father complex." As regards this "childhood neurosis ... [I am] optimistic enough to suppose that humankind will surmount this neurotic phase, just as so many children grow out of their similar neurosis" (1961: 68). This was to occur by means of ever greater consciousness to be achieved through future developments in science and in psychology. Just as a child outgrows its infantile neuroses, advancing civilization would shed the primitive cults and rituals of religion as it grew into adulthood, as it became able to tolerate its heretofore unconscious fears of nature, death, and of other people. As civilization matured, we would outgrow our need for the illusion of an all-powerful father-god as we became able to tolerate the knowledge that our infantile wishes will never be fulfilled: that we will die, that the world does not exist to fulfill our needs.

On the contrary, although Harrison implied throughout her work that she had outgrown the Christianity of her childhood, she did not suggest that religion per se will ever be outgrown. She saw the birth, growth, and death of religions as a cyclic phenomenon, the death of one religion leading, Phoenix-like, to the birth of a new one.

Arnold van Gennep

A more direct influence on the changed perspectives evident in *Themis* was Arnold van Gennep's *The Rites of Passage,* published in 1909. *Themis* opens with a chapter in which she connects an early hymn to Zeus to a male rite of passage. Like van Gennep, Harrison considered adolescent initiation rites to be the most important of all passage rituals. However, where van Gennep focussed almost entirely on male *rites de passage,* Harrison turned her attentions to female *rites de passage,* whose study had until then been almost entirely neglected. She found that these rituals, too, were social in origin and involved a mimetic enactment of death and resurrection, separation and inclusion. Most importantly, they concluded with the adolescent participants being initiated into cultural norms and values by the group elders, in this case by the older women of the community.

Following Durkheim, Harrison stated that in this context, the spirit that emerges from the group ritual is not a god (at least not originally), but rather an expression of communal feeling. When she wrote of Dionysos in *Prolegomena*, Harrison emphasized his foreignness, his ecstasy, his androgyny, his maddening power, and his strong connection to women, who predominated in his cult. She theorized that it was the influence of the women's cult of Dionysos that transformed the Eleusinian Mysteries into the form known in the classical period. But in her later book *Epilegomena*, she stressed the importance of the *thiasos* (the group of celebrants following Dionysos) as actually more significant than the god Dionysos himself:

> It was long a puzzle in Greek religion why Dionysos should always be attended by a *thiasos*, a band of dancing revellers ... this band of revellers of young men dancing was closely paralleled in other cults. Greece had not only Satyrs, it had also Kouretes, Korybantes, Titanes, Seilenoi, Bacchoi ... The riddle was read for Greece by the discovery in Crete of the Hymn to the Kouretes, a ritual hymn containing very early material ... The Kouretes are the young men just come to maturity, just initiated into the fertility dance of their tribe ... are the prototypes of all the Satyrs and Seilenoi ... The cult of the Kouretes was at home in Crete and the great central worship of the Mother goddess ... and the young initiated man becomes the consort of the perennial mother. The Kouretes ... tend the holy child and this is with magical intent, they marry that the land may be fertile, they tend the child that their own children may be nurtured ... In like fashion the religious rites of the Satyrs centre round the Mother Semele, the Phrygo-Thracian Earth goddess, and in like fashion the Satyrs project from their band the arch-satyr Dionysos; the *thiasos* is before the god. (1921: 17–18)

Harrison claimed that the Satyrs, Titans, Bacchoi, and others were not mythic beings, as had been universally understood, but rather that they were all originally groups of youths being initiated into the men's societies of their respective lands (e.g., the Kouretes in Crete). In this revisioning of the cult of Dionysus, Harrison has shown us how completely she has absorbed not only Durkheim's ideas about the social origins of religion, but also van Gennep's contributions about the importance of rites of passage, in this case the rite of initiation.

Henri Bergson

The English translation of Henri Bergson's *L'Évolution Créatrice,* published in France in 1907, appeared in 1911.[10] It seems to have made an almost immediate impact on Harrison. In *Themis* she enthusiastically acknowledged that Bergson's concept of *durée* allowed her to understand the fundamental nature of a mystery god. In her Introduction, Harrison wrote:

> I saw ... how deep was the gulf between Dionysos the mystery-god and that Olympos he might never really enter ... I saw in a word that Dionysos, with every other mystery god, was an instinctive attempt to express what Professor Bergson calls *durée*, that life which is one, indivisible and yet ceaselessly changing. I saw on the other hand that the Olympians, amid all their atmosphere of romance and all their redeeming vices, were really creations of what Professor William James called 'monarchical deism.' Such deities are not an intuitive expression, but a late and conscious representation, a work of analysis, of reflection and intelligence. Primitive religion was not, as I had drifted into thinking, a tissue of errors leading to mistaken conduct: rather it is a web of practices emphasizing particular parts of life, issuing necessarily in representations and ultimately dying out in abstract conceptions. (1974: xii)

That is to say, the early gods, the mystery gods, exemplified by Dionysos, represented *instinctual* feeling and expression of life.

> In the light of *L'Évolution Créatrice, Matière et Mémoire* and *Les Données Immédiates de la Conscience* I had come to see the real distinction between the mystery-god Dionysus and the Olympians. (1974: xiii)

Between *Prolegomena* and *Themis*, Harrison revised her thinking as to the origin of Greek religion. In *Prolegomena*, she saw ritual as sympathetic magic; the important numinous forces were the *keres* and *daimones*, more or less inchoate embodiments of natural forces. In the interval between her two major works, she (temporarily it seems) "had drifted into thinking" that "primitive religion was ... a tissue of errors leading to mistaken conduct" (1974: xii). It appears, however, that she did not persist in this belief, since in *Themis*, she returned to (or never truly left behind) the belief that ritual is based on sympathetic magic. Her reading of Bergson, Durkheim, and Freud seems to have revived her belief in ritual and the profound importance of sympathetic magic.

The novelty in *Themis* is that *keres* and *daimones* have largely dropped out (or are at any rate little mentioned) and that the embodied group feeling of social ritual (the Eniautos-Daimon, the Kouros, Dionysos) comes to dominate. While ritual is still acknowledged as sympathetic magic, the emphasis is now on the group, on the social nature of ritual. In *Themis*, Harrison now also left behind the assertion running throughout *Prolegomena* that "myth is ritual misunderstood," claiming that myth and ritual arise together and function together, at least originally:

> This does not, however, imply, as is sometimes supposed, that ritual is prior to myth; they probably arose together. Ritual is the utterance of an emotion, a thing felt, in *action*, myth in words or thoughts. They arise *pari passu*. The myth is not at first *aetiological*, it does not arise to give a reason; it

> is representative, another form of utterance, of expression. When the emotion that started the ritual has died down and the ritual though hallowed by tradition seems unmeaning, a reason is sought in the myth and it is regarded as aetiological. (1974: 16)

Harrison here identified two distinct functions of myths: the myth that originates at the same time as the ritual it accompanies, and the "aetiological" myth that is created after the "emotion that started the ritual has died down" with its meaning, purpose, and function forgotten.

Harrison now saw that the early gods and the mystery gods, exemplified by Dionysos, represented *instinctual* feeling and expression of life. Bergson's concept of *durée* suggested an endless, undying, and ever-evolving life force. But where Bergson's *durée* was a disembodied idea, Harrison saw it embodied in the mystery god Dionysus. Harrison transformed Bergson's concept of *durée* by transferring it to the study of Greek religion and giving it form.[11]

THEMIS AND ANCIENT ART AND RITUAL

In 1912 Harrison published her second great work, *Themis*, a lengthy, academic book that had taken her four years to write. Its inception was occasioned by a trip to Athens she made with Cornford in 1904. During the return trip they stopped off in Crete, where she saw a recently excavated *stele* [standing grave marker] from the temple of Diktaian Zeus in Palaikastro. This *stele*, dating from the second or third century AD, was inscribed with a hymn to Zeus, called the "hymn of the *Kouretes*." This hymn describes the dancing ritual of a band of young men (the *Kouretes*) who are the companions of Zeus. They dance and sing for fertility and "for goodly Themis." The *stele* with its inscription made a deep impression on Harrison; she dwelt on trying to understand its meaning over the following years. It was only after this lengthy incubation that she came to her understanding of it. The result was *Themis*.

The ritual that so intrigued Harrison was dedicated to the goddess Themis, whose name means literally "that which is set down," and by extension "law." But as a personified goddess, Themis has a vastly more significant purview. She embodies something more like the Universal Order of Nature and of All Things. No wonder Harrison chose to name her book in tribute to this powerful energy.

Harrison was now interested in showing how religion arises from the spirit of group feeling, as exemplified in Greek religion by the initiation rite of the dancing *Kouretes,* described in the *stele* of Palaikastro. She now saw the Diktaian Zeus, for whom the *Kouretes* dance, not as a god as we understand the term today (or as Greeks of the classical age understood the term), but rather as an expression of the group spirit of the band of youths being initiated in their dance ritual. Harrison's new emphasis on the social origin of Greek religion builds on ideas that she had absorbed over the previous decade from her reading of Durkheim, van Gennep, and Bergson. She saw the Diktaian Zeus of the Palaikastro *stele* not as the patriarchal god of the Homeric epics, but rather as the group projection (a "group-daimon") of the youthful dancing *Kouretes*. Harrison was here building on the concept of initiation as developed by van Gennep in his *The Rites of Passage* (1909).

Whereas *Prolegomena* was Harrison's attempt to excavate the chthonic prehistory of Greek religion, in *Themis* she presented nothing less than a general theory for the origin of all religions. In *Prolegomena,* Harrison proposed that the Greek gods and goddesses evolved from inchoate, chthonic *daimones* and bodiless *keres,* but in *Themis* Harrison left these behind. She drew support for her sociological theory from noting that, in art and literature Dionysos was generally presented surrounded by his *thiasos*, his band of maddened, revelling worshippers. She saw Dionysos's identity as endless life (*zoë*), as an embodiment of Bergson's *durée*. Both *zoë* and the *thiasos* were central to Dionysos's identity:

> I saw why Dionysos, the mystery-god, who is the expression and representation of *durée*, is, alone among Greek divinities, constantly attended by a thiasos, a matter cardinal for

> the understanding of his nature. The mystery-god arises out of those instincts, emotions, desires which attend and express life; but these emotions, desires, instincts, in so far as they are religious, are at the outset rather of a group than of individual consciousness. (1974: xiii)

The *thiasos* of Dionysos, like the group of *Kouretes* engaged with Diktaian Zeus, come together for their rite, their *dromenon*. Harrison saw the dance of the *Kouretes* as commemorating and anticipating the New Birth of Diktaian Zeus. She connected this rite of Zeus to those associated with Dionysos:

> The *dromenon* in its sacral sense is, not merely a thing done, but a thing *re*-done, or *pre*-done with magical intent. The magical dance of the Kouretes is a primitive form of the dromenon, it commemorates or anticipates, in order magically to induce, a New Birth. The Dithyramb, from which the drama arose, was also a *dromenon*, of the New Birth. In the drama then we may expect to find survivals of a ritual akin to that of the Kouretes. Further, the *dromenon* is a thing which, like the drama, is collectively performed. Its basis or kernel is a *thiasos* or *choros*. (1974: xv)

Harrison sees the sacrificial rites of the major festivals of Greek religion as all arising from the same root: spring *dromena* having the "magical intent of the renewal of the year ... conceived of as a conflict, dramatic setting forth of the natural happening of the spring. This *drama* might with equal appropriateness be represented as a Death followed by a Rebirth or as a contest followed by a victory" (1974: xvi). These *dromena*, or "magical rites of spring" expressed in conflict include not only the Dionysian rite of the *dithyramb*, but also the *agones* (athletic games) and the *drama* (tragedy and comedy), tragedy having grown out of the *dithyramb*. This explains why Harrison asked Cornford to write a section on the athletic games for *Themis* and Murray to contribute a chapter on tragedy, which he called "Excursus on the Ritual Forms Preserved in Greek Drama."

An idea central to *Themis* is the figure of the *eniautos daimon.* This "year daimon" or "year spirit" is similar to "vegetation spirit" but is larger in scope, including not only the annual cycle of the grain harvest, but also the fertility of all nature: animals, plants, humans. Moreover, Harrison's *eniautos daimon* is not an independently existing spiritual being, but rather a projection of the group spirit, a "group-daimon." She acknowledges her debt to Frazer and Mannhardt's "Tree-Spirit, Corn-Spirit, Vegetation-Spirit," but she finds their terms to be inadequate to fully communicate the group feeling so central to the seasonal *dromenon* (ritual) she is describing, its engagement with "the whole world-process of decay, death, renewal" (1974: xvi). She acknowledged that in drama and in some rituals the *eniautos daimon* might take on the name of a hero, but insisted that the hero, or the protagonist of a tragedy, is merely a mask disguising the underlying reality of the seasonal group-daimon, the *eniautos daimon.*

One year after *Themis* was published, Harrison came out with *Ancient Art and Ritual,* in which she presented the ideas of *Themis* even more clearly and succinctly. The "art" in the title refers largely to *drama,* to theatrical performance. From the beginning, she states that art and ritual are "two divergent developments [that] have a common root, and that neither can be understood without the other. It is at the outset one and the same impulse that sends a man to church and to the theatre" (2007: 2). This is a remarkable break from her earlier statement that "myth is ritual misunderstood" (Verrall 1890: iii). She is now saying that myth, rather than being a misunderstanding of ritual, instead arises from the same root as ritual and grows out of it. In *Ancient Art and Ritual* Harrison uses the term "art" to refer only to theatrical drama (and not to the vases, reliefs, and sculptures otherwise so important to her) and to mean by "myth" those myths revisioned by the tragedians that were performed on stage as part of a Dionysian ritual.

Harrison believes that ritual (*dromenon*) originated as sympathetic magic, an acting out by the group of the thing desired (rain, fertility, success in hunting or war). Ritual is mimetic, an enactment of the fulfillment of the desired outcome; it is a form of sympathetic magic. She introduces numerous examples drawn from Frazer of how rituals and dances are so often done as a group.

Harrison takes care to insist that rituals are not spontaneous acts or one-time acts of strong emotion, nor are they imitations of a thing desired. They are not acts carried out by a solitary person. According to her definition, a ritual must be communal and must arise from an "emotional tension" such as the desire for food or for offspring (2007: 18). Rituals are necessarily recurrent, and most often recur annually (2007: 26–28). Moreover, rituals originate in *mimesis*. For Harrison ritual *mimesis* is not simply "imitation" of the thing desired, whether the hunted animal, success in war, rain, or the growth of crops, but rather the "acting out" of that thing. The ritual *mimesis* of a hunt would not be simply the imitation of a desired animal, but an acting out of the hunt and of the animal being pursued and killed in the hunt (2007: 24–25). This somewhat unusual definition of ritual *mimesis* as a form of acting, already intimates that she sees ritual as evolving into *drama*.

Here, for Harrison, desire and emotion are the primary motivation for ritual and art: "Art and ritual, though perhaps not wholly ritual, spring from the incomplete cycle, from unsatisfied desire, from perception and emotion that have somehow not found immediate outlet in practical action" (2007: 21). Prominent examples are hunger, aggression, and the desire for rain, fertility, and success in war and the hunt. These group emotions find their "immediate outlet in practical action," that is, in rituals such as dances and *dromena*: mimetic actings-out or pantomimes. So far, Harrison has not strayed far from what others have theorized about the origins of ritual, but now she asserts a new idea: because many of these rituals recur periodically at set times, often annually, they no longer occur spontaneously when the group emotion or need arises. "Ritual acts ... which depend on the periodicity of the seasons are acts necessarily delayed" (2007: 28). This periodicity and lack of spontaneity result in a weakening of emotional power underlying the ritual. The "group *daimon*," the emotional power of the social group arising from such rituals, becomes detached from the ritual itself and becomes weaker over time. Simultaneously the annual repetition of the ritual results in the group *daimon* coming to be embodied as a god: "[T]hese periodic festivals are the stuff on which those faded, unaccomplished actions and desires which we call gods—Attis, Osiris, Dionysos—are made" (2007: 29). Harrison settles on Dionysos as the exemplar of such a god that arose from annual spring festivals of death and fertility: "a conception, a kind of *daimon*, or spirit, is fashioned, who lives and dies again in a perpetual cycle. The periodic festival begets a kind of not immortal, but perennial, god" (2007: 40).

Harrison's discussion raises a paradox that she does not resolve. On the one hand the ritual, which initially expressed group emotion and which engendered the "group *daimon*," when repeated annually becomes detached from spontaneously felt group emotion and over time loses its emotional power. Simultaneously, as the group ritual's emotional power becomes weaker the group *daimon* comes to be embodied as a god. Yet the Olympian deities were seen as powerful and immortal, not as "faded ... desires which we call gods." How are we to square this vision of Dionysos as a "faded desire" with the powerfully numinous Dionysos Harrison presented to us in the latter half of *Prolegomena*? She never quite explains this.

Harrison's later view that the gods derive from the group *daimon* of ritual is markedly different from the Euhemerism she presented in *Prolegomena*, where she asserted that male gods are merely divinized heroes, the heroes themselves being merely heroized ancestors. Expanding on Bergson and Durkheim, she now sees gods as arising from the group spirit of rituals, especially ritual dances. For example, Harrison writes that Dionysos has his origin in the annually repeated ritual and the group *daimon* that gave rise to it: "Dionysos, the Bull-God, is but the actual holy Bull himself, or rather the succession of annual holy Bulls once perceived, then remembered, generalized, conceived" (2007: 58–59). In *Prolegomena*, Harrison had understood Dionysos to be an immigrant god, coming from Thrace associated with a foreign, utterly un-Greek form of mystery religion. However, in *Themis* she offers entirely new theories for the origin of this god: he is the group *daimon* of the dancing youths, the leader of this dancing group ritual, and the sacrificial animal itself.

Dionysos is the god of spring and fertility, rebirth and immortality, of the bull and the goat-song. He is the the *kouros*, the group *daimon* arising from the *dithyramb*: "the god who arose out of the rite, the dromenon of tribal initiation, the rite of the new, the second birth. He is Dionysos. His name, according to recent philology, tells us—Dionysos, the 'Divine Young Man'" (2007: 65).

In the later chapters of *Themis*, Harrison explores the evolution from ritual to art, that is, from *dromenon* to *drama*. The etymologic origin of these two words is the same, they both mean essentially "deed" or "thing done," however, their meanings have diverged over time and with usage. *Dromenon* came to have the connotation of "rite" while *drama* evolved toward the meaning it has for us today: theatrical performance. The *dromena* of Greek religion Harrison presents as examples in *Themis* are dancing rites: the Dance of the Kouretes and the *dithyramb*. The *dithyramb* was a springtime ritual of dance and song dedicated to Dionysos, performed by men and boys in a dancing ground called an *orchestra*, in which all present participated. Her primary example of the evolution from ritual to art, from *dromenon* to *drama*, is that of the evolution from Dionysian *dithyramb* to the tragedies performed at the Athenian Dionysia.

Harrison understands the *dithyramb* as an initiation (literally, a "going-in") ritual of young men (*epheboi*), who were "going in" to manhood. This interpretation relies on a questionable etymology of the word *dithyramb*, which is now believed to be of non-Indo-European origin. Harrison believes "Dithyrambos ... is the Divine Leaper, Dancer, and Lifegiver" (2007: 59). Again, citing numerous examples from Frazer's *The Golden Bough*, she makes the astute observation that these initiation rituals of young men are often characterized by a death and rebirth. The initiates are termed "twice-born," their first birth being to their mothers and into the world of women, while their second birth is from their fathers and into the world of men. In support of her theory, she notes Dionysos's two births: the first from his earthly mother Semele, and the second from the thigh of his divine father Zeus.

According to Aristotle's *Poetics,* tragedy originated from the *dithyramb* (2001: 1458). But whereas *dromena* with rituals such as the *dithyramb* are performed by the entire group for a practical purpose arising from group emotion, *drama* is performed by only a small sub-group, the larger group having now become non-participant observers. Moreover, the *drama* does not arise from group (or personal) emotion: "[T]he dromenon, the thing actually done by yourself has become a drama, a thing also done, but abstracted from your doing" (2007: 74). While ritual and art may appear outwardly similar, the distinction between them is that ritual serves a practical purpose and art does not:

> Ritual ... was a re-presentation or a pre-presentation ... a copy or imitation of life, but, —and this is the important point,—always with a practical end. Art is also a representation of life and the emotions of life, but cut loose from immediate actions ... The end of art is in itself. Its value is not mediate but immediate. (2007: 78)

Ritual "mediates" between the group and nature; it impels nature by sympathetic magic. Drama is "immediate" and what happens on the stage directly affects the observers.

In Harrison's view, the weakening of the power of ritual in Greek religion began with the emergence of gods from the group *daimon* of ritual, which resulted in "those faded, unaccomplished actions and desires which we call gods" (2007: 29). A further weakening occurred in the transition from ritual to art, from *dromenon* to *drama,* from active participation to observed spectacle. Coincident with these changes, the Greeks were also beginning to lose faith in their ability to manipulate nature by recourse to the sympathetic magic of ritual. Mythology and sacrifice began to replace the participatory, mimetic ritual of sympathetic magic, such as the dance of the *dithyramb*: "So the dromenon, the thing done, wanes, the prayer, the praise, the sacrifice waxes. Religion moves away from drama toward theology, but the ritual mould of the dromenon is left ready for a new content" (2007: 82).

In her assertion that "religion move[d] away from drama," that drama became mere spectacle, Harrison appears to set aside Aristotle's observation of the numinous power of tragedies, their power to effect a catharsis of the primary emotions, pity and fear.

In *Prolegomena* and her earlier work, Harrison hewed closely to William Robertson Smith's line that myth was decidedly secondary to ritual. She emphasized then that myth was "ritual practice misunderstood" (Verrall 1890: iii). However, by the time she wrote *Themis* this dismissive attitude disappears. In its place, she understands myth to be not a misunderstanding of ritual, but something added to an older ritual as it evolves into a newer ritual as theatrical drama, after the people have lost their belief in the power of the older ritual's sympathetic magic. The myth carries the spoken meaning of the new ritual. As the myth-less ritual of the *dithyramb* becomes the spectacle of tragedy, it takes on myths derived from Homer. Harrison no longer considers myth secondary to ritual but rather that "[t]he primary meaning of myth in religion is just the same as in early literature; it is the spoken correlative of the acted rite, the thing done; it is τὸ λεγόμενον [to legomenon] as contrasted with or rather as related to τὸ δρώμενον [to dromenon]" (1974: 328).

In the long-running argument about whether myth or ritual was primary, Harrison initially stood firmly as a "ritualist," insisting that ritual was primary and that myth arose only later, when the original, magical meaning of ritual had been forgotten. In her later work, Harrison came to view myth and ritual as functioning together, one informing the other.

NOTES

1. Strictly speaking, ritualism refers simply to the study of rituals. However, in the nineteenth and early twentieth centuries, the term refers to the efforts of academics such as Harrison and the Cambridge Ritualists, Robertson Smith, and Frazer to emphasize the importance of ritual

over intellectual aspects of religion such as creed, dogma, and theology. Ritualism in this period frequently dealt with the fraught question of the priority of ritual vs. myth. It had been supposed that ritual, as in the Christian Eucharistic Mass, was the acting out of a myth. However, Harrison agreed with Robertson Smith and Frazer that ritual preceded myth. Today, this question has largely been side-stepped and most scholars of ritual agree simply that myth and ritual go together and that the question of priority of the one over the other cannot be answered in any general sense.

2. Although his ideas of cultural evolution and "survivals" are no longer supported, E. B. Tylor (1832–1917) is considered the founder of cultural evolution. Terms such as "primitives" and "savages" that are no longer considered appropriate, were usual at the time.
3. Smith here gives in a somewhat different form, the earliest expression of what was to become Harrison's famous dictum: "myth is ritual misunderstood."
4. Nietzsche's ideas were on everyone's mind in the 1890s, even among those who had not read his works. Nietzsche's *Thus Spake Zarathustra* (1883), filled with the gnomic utterances, myths, and allegories of Nietzsche's mystical prophet, exerted enormous influence in the intellectual climate of nineteenth-century Europe. His ideas were "in the air." Harrison acknowledged her intellectual debt to Nietzsche. From him she absorbed the "hermeneutics of suspicion," as it was later to be called (a hermeneutics that has become so prominent in the twentieth and twenty-first centuries), and applied this to the study of Greek religion.
5. Harrison's expression of the ideas of Durkheim is exemplified in a quote from her essay "Unanimism and Conversion," contained in her book *Alpha and Omega*:

> [Religion] is not the aspiration of the individual soul after a god, or after the unknown, or after the infinite; rather it is the expression, utterance, projection of the emotion, the desire of a group. Now, historically this is true of the genesis of religion ... Religion, in its rise, is indistinguishable from social custom, embodying social emotion. (1915: 50–51)

Durkheim's detection of social patterns appealed to Harrison's aesthetic sensibilities:

> [T]o her the psychological fragmentation that resulted from the rationalistic view of religion as seen in Frazer must have been distinctly unsatisfactory from an aesthetic point of view. In this case, rationalism explains away, rather than explains, and leaves the phenomena

> unaccounted for. She must have seen Durkheim's view of religion as a projection of group needs and wishes as not only in tune with her own intuitions but unifying rather than atomizing and therefore more likely to be right: it was her "desire to see a pattern." (This of course does not mean that she did not believe Durkheim in fact to be correct, in an intellectual sense; only that she must have felt assured he was right because of the elegance with which so many kinds of phenomena were brought together and illuminated.) (Ackerman 1991b: 78)

6. In 1913, Freud published *Totem and Taboo* (1950), a collection of four previously published essays (appearing in 1912 and 1913 in *Imago*). This early work represents Freud's first exhaustive exposition of his psychological theories of religion. His theories encompass projections of the parental (especially paternal) *imago* (image/likeness), elements of obsessional neurosis, and the Oedipus complex. He identified tabooed objects and behaviors among his neurotic patients, especially those with obsessional neurosis, and traced the roots of this taboo to sexual anxieties. In his exploration of totemism, he recalls the identifications of children with animals side by side with their phobias toward them. In this, he sees the roots of totemistic identification of societies with various animals. He will later expand on many of these ideas in later volumes such as *Moses and Monotheism* (1967) (in which he reprises the theme of patricide) and *The Future of an Illusion* (1927).

   The concept of taboo pervades Harrison's writings. The ambivalence of feeling inherent in the Anthesteria, the simultaneity of joyful drinking with the fear and purgation of ancestral ghosts and *keres*, emerges from the tabooed, magical nature of wine, the *pharmakon* at the center of this festival. On the one hand wine gives joy, while on the other it contains spirits (in both senses of the word). It provides nourishment even as it causes the sickness of inebriation and death by hepatic cirrhosis. Harrison identified the taboos of Greek religion as present predominantly in the religion of the chthonic stratum as well as in the mysteries. Ambivalence is the very essence of taboo. Whereas a totem is the physical embodiment of ambivalence, taboo is its societal instantiation, its enactment. In both totem and taboo, holiness and pollution are conjoined.

   Both Harrison and Freud laid heavy emphasis on the phenomenon of taboo in their studies of religion. While their respective understandings of the workings of taboo are similar, they see the origins of taboo very differently. They both acknowledge Frazer's working definition of taboo in *The Golden Bough*:

   > To us various classes ... appear to differ totally in character and condition; some of them we should call holy, others ... unclean and pol-

> luted. But the savage makes no such moral distinction between them; the conceptions of holiness and pollution are not yet differentiated in his mind ... they are dangerous and in danger, and the danger ... is what we should call spiritual or ghostly. (1996: 260)

But whereas Harrison maintains an expansive understanding of taboo as it underlies religion, Freud understands it much more narrowly, attributing the origin of taboo to the particular ambivalent emotions that underlie the Oedipus complex.

In *Prolegomena,* written ten years before Freud's *Totem and Taboo*, Harrison denied the special relationship between gods and the animals sacrificed to them, upon which Freud insisted. To give but one example, she points out that the animal sacred to Athena, the owl, was never sacrificed to her. Wolves were not sacrificed to Apollo, eagles were not sacrificed to Zeus.

7. Freud agreed with Bachofen that the religion of the "Minoan-Mycenean" Goddess was left behind historically, but the "Minoan Mycenean" layer of consciousness as an aspect of the psyche is never abandoned. For males, it underlies the Oedipus complex. For women this primary bond persists more as identification with their mothers, but this too is never truly left behind (Downing 2004: 64). Our profound, ongoing desire for return to the state of primary narcissism, of primary union with the mother, is reflected in our search for "peace, harmony, resolution, completion, to what [Freud] calls the death drive" (Downing 2018: 265). In Freud's view, the search to return to primary narcissism is the foundation of mysticism, of the mystic's search for oneness, wholeness, and union with God.

Harrison's mother died giving birth to her, but Freud's mother survived into old age. Freud seems to have idealized his mother, as Harrison did her birth mother. Perhaps because he was the favorite son of the beloved mother Freud was unable to recognize the ambivalence of his feelings toward her, whereas he was able to recognize the ambivalence he felt in respect to his father, especially after his father's death. For both Harrison and Freud, this lack of ambivalence toward the idealized mother may provide a basis for their response to goddess-images. Downing suggests that "[Freud] explicitly likens the discovery of this earliest childhood period to the discovery by Bachofen of the Minoan-Mycenean period in Greek religious history when goddesses were more important than the gods" (Downing 2018: 266–67).

Freud tells us that this phase of union with the mother is something that we necessarily outgrow with the emergence of consciousness and the awareness of separation, but to which we yearn to return throughout life.

8. A valorization of the feminine also clearly plays a strong role in Freud's psychology. In the tremendous importance he gave to infantile and childhood experience in the development of the psyche, the role of the mother is fundamental. The father certainly has an important role, but this is later and of secondary importance. The mother's role is earlier and always more foundational. Even as Freud recognized the greater importance of woman as mother in the development of the psyche, he emphasized the later importance of the father as protector, object of aggression, and thus of guilt feelings. Freud sees the father as the desired savior and protector from the overwhelming forces of the world (Freud 1950: 183; 2013: 11). He sees the idealized father as the source of the God-image (Freud 1961: 21, 28, 38, 54), even as he envisions the origin of the Goddess-image in the phase of primary narcissism (Downing 2018: 266).
9. In the Oedipus complex, the mother is the ultimate femme fatale, mother and lover, bringer of life and bringer of death. However, because the father stands between the child and the mother, especially between the male child and his mother, he comes to be resented as an obstacle to the mother's love. So it is the patricidal aspect of the Oedipus complex that Freud associates with the origin of religion (Freud 1950: 176–77; 1967: 103).
10. The influence of this book in the early decades of the twentieth century was enormous. According to Harrison's memoir, it was one of the three most important books in her intellectual development (along with Aristotle's *Ethics* and Freud's *Totem and Taboo*) (Harrison 1926: 80). The idea of "vitalism," which was current in the latter part of the nineteenth century and was picked up by many thinkers, was central not only to the writings of Bergson and Durkheim but by those of Frazer as well. This vitalism courses through Harrison's writings.
11. Bergson's concept of *durée* is notoriously difficult to define and then to translate into English. However, the sense in which Harrison seems to understand it in the above quotation from her introduction to *Themis* sounds very much like Kerényi's use of the Greek work *zoē* (as opposed to *bio*s, another, but very different, Greek word for life). Harrison's understanding of Bergson's *durée* (like Kerényi's use of *zoē*) suggests an endless, undying, and ever-evolving life force.

CHAPTER 4

HARRISON REDISCOVERS THE NUMINOUS

Not only did Harrison rediscover the importance of ritual and reinterpret the relationship of myth to ritual, but she was also one of the earliest scholars to begin the process of honoring the experiential, emotional, and spiritual aspect of Greek religion. In this, she was going against the academic currents of her time, based as they were on a skeptical approach to religion, emphasizing the functional aspects of ritual and myth. She not only observed and described, but seems to have felt for herself the power of the numinous in Greek religion, a power she did not feel in the Christianity of her upbringing. In this, she anticipated by many years such scholars as C. G. Jung and James Hillman, who were also attuned to the living power of religion. While Harrison never claimed to "believe" in the Greek gods and goddesses, in reading *Prolegomena* it is difficult to miss how deeply stirred she was by the Greek goddesses and their ancestresses. Her writings also betray how profoundly moved she was by Dionysos and, even more, by the Orphism of later antiquity. Just as she was beginning to write about Dionysos, she met Gilbert Murray, who was then working on the *Bacchae*, Euripides' play about Dionysos and Dionysian religion. This led her to expand her study of Dionysos in a way that seems to have overtaken her by surprise. As she wrote Murray:

> It's rather dreadful, the whole centre of gravity of the book has shifted. It began as a treatise on Keres with a

> supplemental notice on Dionysus. It is ending as a screed on Dionysus with an introductory talk about Keres. Whose fault is that? *Never, never* again will I ask you to lecture when I am writing a book, a nice sound one too, it was, till last autumn. (qtd. in Ackerman 1991b: xxvii)

It is perhaps not accidental that she should have become overwhelmed by the very god who overwhelmed his devotees (as well as those who resisted him) with divine madness and who moreover, was favored by women.

While Harrison shared in the religious skepticism of her time and in its rejection of Christianity, in *Prolegomena* she presented a fascinating ambivalence as to the deepest functions of religion and its future. She compared the decline represented by the Olympian stage of Greek religion in antiquity to what she observed happening in the Christianity of her time. But she then went on to discover that the demise of the oldest and most profound strata of Greek religion had been only apparent. She discovered that these ancient layers had persisted in women's cults, fertility cults, and mystery cults; when the religion of the Olympian gods and goddesses was in its turn in decline, they re-emerged as revivals of the mystery cults of Eleusis and of Dionysos and in the emergence of Orphism from the cult of Dionysos. These revivals were concerned with the cycle of life, death, and rebirth; the Earth mother, women, fertility, madness, ecstasy, and sexuality. Harrison recognized that because the mystery cults, many of which were of far greater antiquity than the Olympian religion, met a profound ongoing spiritual need, they persisted and then revived even as Olympian religion withered away.

Nearly half of *Prolegomena* is devoted to the cults of Dionysos, Orphism, and the mystery cults. In these pages Harrison was wrestling not only with discovering a history of Greek religion that was mostly factual (yet, to a degree speculative), but also with her own subjective feelings and her own spirituality.

Harrison saw something more in Greek religion than merely the "things done" and "things experienced." She saw that the mystery cults and Orphism altered the Greeks' attitudes toward death and their views of reality. She believed that religion has a function that is not outgrown in the process of cultural evolution, that it is something of great and enduring significance. Harrison was one of the first scholars to transcend the excessively skeptical and functional nineteenth-century attitude toward religion, opening herself to perspectives that would soon be explored by others such as Rudolph Otto and William James: that at the heart of religious experience lies some necessary, yet ineffable experience of reality, that religion is not simply a collection of rituals, stories, and beliefs, but that it arises out of the very core of our being.

One of the issues that religion addresses is our deep-seated fear of death and of non-being. The religion of the Olympian gods offered no comfort to the Greeks as they confronted death. In Homer, the spirit or soul (*psyche)* departs from the body (*soma*) and descends to the Underworld to spend eternity in oblivion as a shade (*skia*). Archaic Greece had no concept of a true afterlife, aside perhaps from the poorly characterized Tartarus [a dark abyss, below even Hades]. There was no divine reward or punishment, certainly no reincarnation. The inscription on the temple of Apollo at Delphi "know thyself" (γνῶθι σεαυτόν) commands not self-knowledge in our modern understanding of the term, but instead commands that we remember that we are mortal.

This attitude began to shift in the late sixth century BC, when a profound change swept through Greece. The cult of Dionysos became more popular and began to influence the Eleusinian Mysteries. At about the same time, it began to give rise to the newer cult of Orphism. Pythagoreanism, with its asceticism, mysticism, and belief in reincarnation, also appeared at this time. The religious current of this later stage of antiquity was characterized by the decline of the Olympian religion and the re-emergence of the cults of the goddesses (especially at Eleusis) and of Dionysos.

HARRISON'S UNDERSTANDING OF DIONYSOS

Dionysos was the strangest of the gods of classical Greece. On one hand, Harrison saw him as one of the primitive chthonic deities of the archaic Greeks who, like Demeter, survived what Harrison believed to be both the arrival and the waning of the Olympian gods. Paradoxically, she also believed him to be a recent arrival, as did other nineteenth and early twentieth century scholars: "[I]t is beyond question that Dionysos was a late-comer into Greek religion, an immigrant god, and that he came from that home of spiritual impulse, the North" (Harrison 1991: 364). These assumptions have come under severe scrutiny in more recent years, well after Harrison's death. We now know that Dionysos's name is attested in Greek sites as early as the fifteenth century BC in Linear B inscriptions, perhaps associated with wine (Burkert 1985: 162). Harrison recognized that since Dionysos appears in Homer we know that he must have arrived in Greece prior to the writings of the epics, however "[i]n Homer Dionysos is not yet an Olympian" (Harrison 1991: 365), which Harrison interpreted as supporting his more recent arrival in the Greek mainland. She imagined Dionysos as one of the chthonic deities, associated with veneration of the dead and magical practices associated with vegetal fertility. She saw the cult of Dionysos as persisting through the waning of the Olympian gods, because of the ecstatic, mystical, transformative aspects of his later cult.

Dionysos is unique among the Greek gods in many respects. Not only was he considered by the Greeks to be a foreign god and a late arrival, but the cult of this male god was practiced predominantly by women. Moreover, his androgyny and his blurring of boundaries and distinctions made him seem uncanny. Uniquely among Greek gods, Dionysos was mortal: he died and was resurrected, thus blurring the distinctions between the immortal gods and mortal humans. He was the god of intoxication and divine madness, of mountainside orgies, of the loss of order and propriety. He was the god "who arrives"[1] and who overwhelms, not with the overt external power of a god, but with the more subversive power to inflict madness.

In *Prolegomena*, Harrison considered Dionysos to be the single most important deity in Greek religion. She saw that the religion of the Olympian gods had become enfeebled, due in part to its transactional attitude toward its gods (characterized by *do ut des*: "I give so that you should give") and in part to artistic and poetic depictions of the gods, which made them seem all too human. Into this spiritual void came the (apparently) new religions of Dionysos and Orpheus:

> As man grew more civilized, his image, mirrored in the gods, grew more beautiful and *pari passu* the worship he offered to these gods advanced from 'aversion' (ἀποτροπή) to 'tendance' (θεραπεία). But all along we have been conscious that something was lacking, that even these exquisite presentations of the Nymphs and the Graces, the Mother and the Daughter, are really rather human than divine, that their ritual, whether of ignorant and cruel 'aversion' or of genial 'tendance,' was scarcely in our sense religious. These perfect Olympians and even these gracious Earth-goddesses are not really Lords over man's life who made them, they are not even ghosts to beckon and threaten, they are lovely dreams, they are playthings of his happy childhood, and when full-grown he comes to face realities, from kindly sentiment he lets them lie unburied in the lumber-room of his life. Just when Apollo, Artemis, Athene, nay even Zeus himself, were losing touch with life and reality, fading and dying of their own luminous perfection, there came into Greece a new religious impulse, an impulse really religious, the mysticism that is embodied for us in the two names Dionysos and Orpheus. (Harrison 1991: 363–64)

Harrison is convinced of the importance of Dionysian influences in the Eleusinian Mysteries: "[A]ll in [the Eleusinian Mysteries] that was not a primitive harvest festival, all or nearly all their spiritual significance, was due to elements borrowed from the cult of Dionysos" (1991: 539). Harrison sees the resurgence of the older chthonic gods such as Demeter, with strong influences from supposedly late-arriving Dionysos, as the source of the mystery religions that became popular in classical and late antiquity. (We now recognize that her assertion is open to debate, since earlier "primitive harvest festivals" may well have included ecstatic elements.)

The cult of Dionysos later gave rise to the cult of Orphism, which in turn may have influenced Christianity.[2] Harrison considered the cults of Dionysos and Orpheus to be so closely intertwined as to have been already confused in classical antiquity (1991: 454). It is characteristic of Dionysos's uncanny character and his purported "foreignness" that he was only grudgingly and inconsistently accepted as one of the Olympian gods. Indeed, it is important to acknowledge that Harrison's attitudes to Dionysian religion and to Orphism are somewhat confusing and contradictory, possibly due to incompletely worked-out conflicts in Harrison herself. It seems that before she began work on *Prolegomena*, she considered herself an atheist, but as her work proceeded, she recognized in the cults of the goddesses and of Dionysos something of deep spiritual value to the Greeks (and more indirectly, to herself). Her hostility to Christianity at times expressed itself in hostility to religion in general. This is evident in her denigration of Orphism as a weakened, attenuated form of Dionysian religion, whereas others have viewed the asceticism and heightened spirituality of Orphism as instead a higher development of the cult Dionysos. It is evident that Harrison was moved by the women's cult of Dionysos but given her general rejection of religion as primitive magic ritual, it may be that she had no framework for understanding her own inchoate response. It is tempting to speculate whether, if Harrison had gone more deeply into her own subjective experience of the Dionysian cult, she might have come to agree with Walter Otto, C.G. Jung, and James Hillman that the Greek gods are in some undeniable way real, that they have a reality within the human psyche.

The mystery cults of Demeter and Dionysos do not fit neatly into Harrison's classification of early chthonic and later Olympian religions. She sees Demeter as an ancient chthonic goddess whose cult persisted into the classical era and who thereby became an Olympian goddess. Demeter's pre-Olympian chthonic cult either originated as a mystery cult or evolved into one. Harrison saw Dionysos as a newcomer to Greece who brought his foreign mystery cult with him from the beginning. She saw him as a syncretic god incorporating the Thracian beer-deity Sabazios and the Cretan mystery god Zagreus, who resembled the Egyptian god Osiris. (Harrison 1905: 57; Robinson 2002: 179).[3]

HARRISON'S VIEW OF ORPHISM

In the transition from classical Greek religion to the mystery cults of late classical and Hellenistic Greece, the attitude toward death changed markedly. Where early and classical Greek religion saw the dead existing only as shades in a dark Underworld realm, the later mystery cults express a clear hope for immortality in a vivid afterlife (an attitude that had a strong influence on the development of Christian beliefs). This and the Orphic belief in reincarnation suggest to some scholars the impact of influences coming from outside of Greece: "metempsychosis ... is a speculative doctrine more characteristic of India, which remained a kind of foreign body in the framework of Greek religion" (Burkert 1985: 298).

While we remain uncertain about the details of the mystery cults' rituals, a great deal of written testimony has come down to us about the effects on those who underwent initiation. Harrison believed that these cults were a revival of pre-Olympian, chthonic cults of the dead, that had survived for long centuries beneath the veneer of the superimposed Olympian religion. These chthonic cults, with their placations (*apotrope*) of the dead and of innumerable personified spiritual beings such as Death and Disease, had never truly disappeared, but re-emerged in the classical age in Orphism and in mystery cults like that of Eleusis. The Olympian religion with its gods of the upper world and its *polis*-centered rituals, failed to address the spiritual needs of people facing their uncertainties around death and the afterlife and they provided no sense of personal, emotional, and embodied connection to the divine. Whereas, a central concern of Orphism and the mystery cults was death, and what comes after death.

Although much effort has gone into the attempt to identify the *dromena* ("things done") of the Greek mystery cults, Harrison did not speculate further than the archeological and literary evidence allowed. She explored at length fairly well-known components of the cult of Dionysos: the *sparagmos,* the tearing apart of a live animal (a bull, a goat, or, as she suggests, perhaps originally a human child); the *omophagia,* the ritualistic eating of the raw flesh; the *liknophoria,* the carrying of the first fruits of the harvest in the winnowing-fan, the phallus as fertility symbol, the *hieros gamos* (the sacred wedding), and finally the birth of the god.

While Orphism arose from the cult of Dionysos, it diverged markedly in many ways from its parent. Whereas the cult of Dionysos was female-dominated and characterized by sensual excess, animality, and earthiness, Orphism was male-dominated and was characterized by asceticism, spirituality, and otherworldliness.

And yet Harrison saw *omophagia* as paradoxically central to Orphism. While the Orphic cult was characterized by a notable absence of the bloody animal-killings and *omophagia* characteristic of the cult of Dionysos, Harrison saw that the myth of the Titans' killing, dismemberment, and *omophagia* of the infant Dionysos was of central importance to Orphism. The prominence of this myth is striking in a cult known for its asceticism and lack of bloody ritual.

Harrison viewed Orpheus as having been a real, historical person, a reformer of the older Dionysos religion:

> The whole gist of the matter may thus be summed up. Orpheus took an ancient superstition, deep-rooted in the savage ritual of Dionysos, and lent to it a new spiritual significance. The old superstition and the new faith are both embodied in the little Orphic text ... 'Many are the wand-bearers, few are the Bacchoi.' (Harrison 1991: 473)

Harrison identified the radical divergence of Orphism from the mainstream of Greek religion not merely in its promise of an afterlife but in the claim of its initiates to become one with their god. The *epoptes* [ones admitted to the highest degrees of the Mysteries] of Orphism claimed to become God:

> The cardinal doctrine of Orphic religion was then the possibility of attaining divine life. It has been said by some that the great contribution of Dionysos to the religion of Greece was the hope of immortality it brought. Unquestionably the Orphics believed in a future life, but this belief was rather a corollary than of the essence of their faith. Immortality, immutability, is an attribute of the gods ... To become a god was therefore incidentally as it were to attain immortality. But one of the beautiful things in Orphic religion was that the end completely overshadowed the means. Their great concern was to become divine now. That could only be attained by perfect purity. They did not so much seek purity that they might become divinely immortal, they needed immortality that they night become divinely pure. (1991: 477)

In the Olympian stage of Greek religion, as seen in the Homeric epics, the only existence after death was the dark, pitiable existence of the shades in the Underworld. To desire anything more than what was allotted to a person was the supreme crime of *hubris* (1991: 473). The aspiration of a mortal to deity and immortality was unthinkable. While rare individuals had become cult heroes who could be consulted at their graves, none became a god. (The few beings who were divinized, such as Herakles and Asklepios, were already semi-divine by birth.) Orphism took on from Dionysian religion the experience of becoming one with the god, *en theos* (the origin of the English "enthusiasm").

Harrison saw in Orphism the origin of monotheism in Greek religion. She believed that although in Orphism Eros is prominent, Hades, Zagreus, Phanes, and even Zeus are all seen as one god who is ultimately Dionysos. Eukles and Euboleus are but other names for this same god in Orphism, as Bromios, Braites, and Sabazios (gods of cereal intoxication), Nyktelios, "he of the night," and Isodaites, "he of the shared feast" had been earlier, alternative names of Dionysos (1991: 480–81). The various names of the gods represent the variety of faces, moods, and attitudes of the one god: Dionysos. In Orphism, even Zeus comes to be conflated with Dionysos Zagreus (1991: 586). Harrison saw that in Crete, Dionysos long pre-dated the arrival of the Greek god Zeus (1991: 496), and although in Olympian religion the late-arriving Zeus came to overshadow Dionysos Zagreus:

> In the myth of Zagreus, coming to us as it does through late authors, the child is all important, the mother only present by implication. Zeus the late comer has by that time ousted Dionysos in Crete. The mythology of Zeus, patriarchal as it is through and through, lays no stress on motherhood. Practically the Zeus of the later Hellenism has no mother. But the bull-divinity worshipped in Crete was wholly the son of his mother, and in Crete most happily the ancient figure of the mother has returned after long burial to the upper air. (1991: 496)

In the Cretan mystery religion, from which Dionysos arose, "the god in the mysteries of Zagreus was a bull" (1991: 495) and this Cretan god was very closely associated with the Mother Goddess. In Orphism, Dionysos Zagreus, rather than being overcome by Zeus, came to be conflated with him.

DIONYSOS, ORPHEUS AND THE MOTHER GODDESS

Harrison makes the bold assertion that the cults of both Dionysos and Orpheus originated as cults of the Mother Goddess. She claims that it ought not surprise us that the Orphic cult of a male god, reformed by a male religious leader and consisting largely of male followers, should have originated as the cult of the Mother Goddess since this pattern of evolution has occurred repeatedly and in many places. She observed that in earliest Greek religion the divine family configuration was that of Mother and

Daughter. Only later did the divine Son emerge, as in prehistoric Crete, where the ritual was of the Mother and the Son. In many ancient goddess religions, the Mother's son grows up to become her consort. Later still, Greek religion was characterized by "the Son with only a faded Mother in the background, Bacchos and Semele; next the Son is made the Son of his Father, Bacchos is Dionysos; finally he eclipses his Father and reigns omnipotent as Zeus-Hades" (1991: 498). Ultimately, in classical and Hellenistic Greece the Mother goddess makes her return in the mystery cults, in which "the Mother with the Son as attribute came back from Asia Minor to Greece when in Greece the Mother was but the appendage of the Son" (1991: 498).

This renewed prominence of the Mother goddess is reflected in one of Dionysos's names: Brimos, meaning son of the Mother goddess Brimo. Brimo's name in turn, means "angry, terrifying," she was "an underworld goddess ... the triple goddess Hecate, Thessalian goddess of the underworld ... She is the Thessalian Kore" (1991: 551–52).

The more familiar name for Dionysos, Iacchos, "was defined as referring to the child Dionysos 'at the breast'" (1991: 548). Finally, the prominence of the *liknos*, the winnowing fan in the rites of Dionysos, is explained when we learn that the *liknos* was used as a cradle for infants as well as, figuratively, for separating grain from chaff (and initiates from the uninitiated). The *liknos* carried the newly born Dionysos with the first-fruits, and often a *phallos* [phallus], both being attributes of the god. A *liknos* was held over the head of those being initiated into the cult of Dionysos as well as over the heads of couples being married.

The Orphic cult revived the practice of inhumation burials, replacing the practice of cremation that had entered Greece in the Homeric age. Since the Mother Goddess is an earth goddess and an Underworld deity, inhumation of the dead expresses a belief that death is a return to the mother. Harrison sees in this revival of inhumation burials evidence of reinvigoration of the Mother Goddess cult, relating it to Orphism's revival of the older stratum of chthonic, Greek religion, the religion of the Underworld gods.

According to Harrison, for Orphism, the story of Orpheus and Eurydice's marriage and separation is a distortion of a much older mythic theme: that of the Mother Goddess and her Son/Consort, and her annual *anodos* (rising) and *kathodos* (descent). Harrison conflated Eurydice ("wide-ruler") and Semele (whose name she interprets as meaning, simply "Earth"), viewing both as names of the same Mother Goddess of fertility. Harrison joins these myths by suggesting that over time, the Mother-goddess Semele was given a divine Son and Consort, Dionysos, who went down below the Earth to fetch her, and who later came to dominate the cult of the Mother. The temple of Artemis the Savior at Troezen was said to be the place Semele was brought up from Hades by Dionysos. Harrison believed that here "the cult of Artemis is clearly superimposed over an ancient, perhaps nameless, anyhow forgotten cult of underworld gods. There was probably a cleft at hand and a legend of a rising Earth-goddess" (1991: 603). The Earth-goddess, Semele, was accompanied by her son Dionysos in her annual ascent (*anodos*) through this cleft in the Earth. As the "mantle of Dionysos" descended on Orpheus, the mantle of Semele descended on Eurydice. Over time their ascent began to be accompanied by a descent (*kathodos*).

> Orpheus, priest of Dionysos, took on his resurrection as well as his death; that is the germ from which sprang the beautiful love-story. A taboo-element, common to many primitive stories, is easily added. You may not look back when spirits are about from the underworld. If you do you may have to join them. Underworld rites are often performed 'without looking back.' (1991: 603–4)

Hence the element in the Orpheus and Eurydice myth of Orpheus' backward look. Harrison suggests that for Orphism, Eurydice was a lately renamed Underworld Mother goddess (originally called Semele), and that Orpheus was her Son and Consort. The stories of their descent and ascent to and from the Underworld are later versions of the annual *anodos* and *kathodos* of the Mother Goddess of fertility, incidentally accompanied by her Consort. Semele's descent to Hades is that of Eurydice, which in turn is that of Persephone. Conflation seems to be at the heart of Orphic theology.

Harrison suggests that the Danaides are another survival of the old, chthonic Goddess religion who are revived in Orphism, but in a way that honors their divinity less than that of Eurydice. Harrison identified Orphic vase paintings, in which the Danaides are placed at the lowest level of Hades, signifying that they are being punished for eternity for the crime of murdering their husbands. In Orphism, the Danaides have become representatives of the "uninitiated," a group despised by the Orphic initiates and believed to be deserving of eternal damnation. However, originally the Danaides were

> *well-nymphs* ... watering, fertilizing thirsty Argos ... belong[ing] to the old stratum ... the same stratum as Tantalos, as Sisyphos, as Tityos: they are of the old matriarchal order ... Behind the legend we seem to discern, though dimly, the reflection of some shift of old to new, some transition from the matriarchal freedom to patriarchal marriage enactments. (1991: 619–20)

Similarly, in Orphism "the Kouretes and kindred figures ... are all ministers ... of orgiastic deities, of Rhea and of Dionyos ... They are in fact the male correlatives of the Maenads as Nurses" (1991: 499). The Kouretes, the dancing worshippers of the Mother Goddesses, became dancing worshippers of the young male god, who in Crete was Dionysos Zagreus. Other bands of male dancing worshippers of the Mother Goddess and the young god *Kouros* came to be conflated with the Kouretes: the Korybantes of Asia Minor, the Daktyls of Mt. Ida in Crete, the Kabeiroi of Lemnos and Thebes, and the Telchines. Harrison asserts that all of these groups were identical in one additional respect: they were all Titans, whom Harrison identifies as the worshippers and protectors of Dionysos and, importantly, as enemies of the Olympian gods.

Dromena, ("things done") constitute the actions of every ritual, however *drama* ("deed," "act," especially "stage action" or "dramatic enactment") arose only in the cult of Dionysos. Harrison suggests that this is because

> the real impulse to the drama lay not wholly in "goat-songs" and "circular dancing places" but also in the cardinal, the essentially dramatic, conviction of the religion of Dionysos, that the worshipper can not only worship, but can become, can *be,* his god. Athene and Zeus and Poseidon have no drama because no one, in his wildest moments, believed he could become and be Athene or Zeus or Poseidon. It is indeed only in the orgiastic religions that these splendid moments of conviction could come, and, for Greece at least, only in an orgiastic religion did the drama take its rise. (1991: 568)

Harrison thus saw that in the Dionysian cult, acting out the actions of the god allowed the god's worshippers to *become* the god. The cultic rites of Athene, Zeus, and Poseidon consisted of *dromena* but they were not characterized by *drama,* that is by theater. However, something close to *drama* was present in the rites of one cult besides that of Dionysos: the Eleusinian Mysteries. Harrison states that "[i]n the rites at Eleusis of which most details are known we have the very last stage of the development before the final step was actually taken, we have [dromena] on the very verge of *drama*" (1991: 568). She quotes the author Psellus, who provides a detailed, step-by-step description of the *dromena* of the Eleusinian Mysteries. Not only are the actions described, but so also are the words that are spoken: "I have eaten from the timbrel, I have drunk from the cymbals, I have carried the *kernos,* I have gone down into the bridal chamber." She also quotes Galen as saying: "Lend me then your whole attention even more than you did supposing you were initiated in the Eleusinian and Samothracian mysteries or any other holy rite and give yourself up wholly *to the things done and the things spoken* by the Hierophants" (1991: 569).

Harrison makes the controversial assertion that the deep spiritual value of the Eleusinian Mysteries was due to the late entry into them of elements of the cult of Dionysos. She points out that

> the rites of Eleusis were primarily rites of a harvest festival, that the ceremonies consisted of elaborate purification and fasting, followed by the removal of the taboo on first-fruits, and the consequent partaking of the sacred *kykeon* and the handling of certain sacred objects ... all in [the Eleusinian Mysteries] that was not a primitive harvest festival, all or nearly all their spiritual significance, was due to elements borrowed from the cult of Dionysos. (1991: 539)

However, Harrison's enthusiasm for Orphism was not wholehearted. In places in her evaluation of Orphism, her ambivalence toward religion comes into view. Thus, her attitude toward Orphism sounds at times suspiciously like her attitude toward the evangelical Christianity that was forced on her in her girlhood. Like Plutarch and Plato, she rejected what she terms the "lower aspects" of Orphism:

> Formalism, faddism, priggishness, a constant, and it would seem inevitable lapse into arid symbolism, pseudo-science, pseudo-philosophy, the ignorant revival of obsolete rites, the exhibition of all manner of ignoble thaumaturgy and squalid credulity. (1991: 658)

In addition to the "priggishness" of its asceticism and what she saw as the degradation of its ritual practices into those resembling magic, she abhorred the lower aspects of Orphism's tendencies to excessive, harsh moralism with the accompanying tendency to veer from personal purification into a desire for exacting vengeance in the afterlife of the Underworld, wishing that the uninitiated suffer eternal punishment in an afterlife resembling the Christian Hell (1991: 612). She quotes Plutarch's *On Superstition*: "these are the sort of things that make men atheists, the incantations, wavings and enchantments and magic, runnings round and tabourings, *unclean purifications*, filthy cleansing, barbarous and outrageous penances in sanctuaries, and bemirings" (qtd. in 1991: 516). She also notes Plato's statement in the *Republic*:

> [S]eers and mendicant quacks besiege rich men's doors, exhibiting books by Musaeus and Orpheus ... and in accordance with these they perform sacrifices, inducing not only individual persons but whole cities to believe that you can obtain freedom and purification from sins, while you are still alive, by sacrifices and performances that might please a child, and that there are things they call "rites," which will release us from suffering after we are dead, and that if we do not perform then, then there are fearful things in store for us. (qtd. in 1991: 517)

Harrison also enjoys quoting extensively from Aristophanes' *The Clouds*, with its heavy-handed burlesque of Orphism.

However, Harrison also recognized that despite their misgivings, both Plutarch and Plato were influenced by Orphism, Plato most deeply. Despite her own misgivings about the negative, popular side of Orphism and the abuses to which it was prone, she too found herself attracted to it: "the expression of [Orphism's] highest faith, of a faith so high that it may be questioned whether any faith, ancient or modern, has ever out-passed it" (1991: 586). This should perhaps not come as a surprise given her identification of Orphism with the revival of all that she found most profoundly alive and real in Greek religion: the ancient, pre-Olympian gods of the Underworld, most especially the goddesses. Beyond its emphasis on purification and immortality, Orphism re-established the emphasis of the older stratum of Greek religion, on the Underworld as the home of the gods and goddesses.

On the basis of her examination of vase paintings, Harrison describes the Underworld as a kind of inverted Olympus. Hades and Persephone are enthroned in the central palace. Orpheus is always present, of course, as are the Judges of Hades: Triptolemos, Aiakos, and Rhadamanthys (the brother of Minos, king of Crete), in addition to Herakles (with Cerberus) and Theseus. Interestingly, two figures who were considered enemies of the Olympian gods, and imagined as subject to eternal punishment, are seen by the Orphics as divine beings: Tantalos and Sisyphos. Harrison postulates that both had been real kings who became divinized heroes after death. They were seen as enemies of the Olympian gods not because of outrages committed against them, but simply because they were chthonic beings of the earlier Greek religion. She identifies Sisyphos as "theosophos," the "divinely wise," rather than as a criminal deserving of eternal punishment (1991: 608). Moreover, she suggests that the myth of Sisyphos eternally rolling the stone is a distortion of his original identity as a sun-god, eternally rolling the "large, red-hot stone: its rising and setting might very fitly be represented as the heaving of such as stone up the steep of heaven, whence it eternally rolls back" (1991: 609). Overcoming her ambivalence, and almost in spite of herself, she writes:

> [T]he last word in Greek religion was said by the Orphics, and the beautiful figure of Orpheus is strangely modern. Then, as now, we have, for one side of the picture, a revived and intensified spirituality, an ardent, even ecstatic enthusiasm, a high and self-conscious standard of moral conduct, a deliberate simplicity of life; abstinence from many things, temperance in all, a great quiet of demeanor, a marvelous gentleness to all living things. (1991: 658)

and

> Through all the chaos of his cosmogony and the shifting, uncertain outlines of his personifications, we feel, in these two gods [Bacchus and Eros] lies the real advance of the religion of Orpheus—an advance, not only beyond the *riddance* of ghosts and sprites and demons, but also beyond the gracious and beautiful *service* of those magnified

> mortals, the Olympians. The religion of Orpheus *is* religious in the sense that it is the worship of the real mysteries of life, of potencies [daimones] rather than personal gods [theoi]; it is the worship of life itself in its supreme mysteries of ecstasy and love. (1991: 657)

Although in 1903 when *Prolegomena* was published, Harrison's assertions of the reality of numinous experiences in Greek religion went against the mainstream currents of academic thinking, we may today see her writings as reflecting other, earlier movements of nineteenth-century thought, specifically German Romanticism. Harrison's realization of the numinosity present in Greek religion may reflect a discovery made earlier by German scholars such as Friedrich and Augustus Schlegel, and above all by German Romantic poets such as Hölderlin and Novalis,[4] discoveries taken up by Karl Kerényi and Walter Otto and later still, by James Hillman.

Kerényi, who cited Harrison in writing of the Eleusinian Mysteries, outlines an approach to a psychological understanding of the mysteries suggesting that the mother's search for the daughter, as well as the daughter's search for the mother, on a psychological level represent both a search for and a finding of the self.

> [The initiates] had entered into the role of the Goddess searching for her daughter; they were prepared in the same way as Demeter herself ... Men and women alike appeared in the role of the Goddess searching for her daughter, for a part of herself in her daughter ... The separation of Mother and Daughter, the yearning of Demeter for her own girl-child, the Kore, must be characteristic of undivided human existence, of men as well as women, but in one way of men and in another of women. (Kerényi 1967: 145–46)

Both men and women long for and seek out psychological wholeness. In later Greece this occurred through participation in mystery religions, in which initiates vicariously participated in Demeter's search for Persephone. The goddess who was originally one had become two, mother and daughter, reflecting the sense of division that occurs in our psyches during the transition from childhood to adulthood. The psyche becomes divided when ego consciousness emerges from the (maternal) unconscious; the ego must then search for the part of itself that it has "lost," a part that is perceived as the "lost feminine."

Erich Neumann[5] also cited Harrison's emphasis on the feminine. Like Jung, Neumann sees the unconscious as having an essentially feminine character, with both "elementary" and "transformative" components. He sees the emergence of the conscious ego as a masculine principle (in both sexes) that, after arising from the feminine unconscious, then proceeds to overlay and negate it (1994: 251–65; 2015: 147–48). He saw the unconscious not only as existing prior to, but also as vastly larger and more powerful than ego-consciousness. Neumann's image of the feminine unconscious as mother of the masculine ego consciousness, which once born proceeds to dominate, ignore, and erase the maternal unconscious, is remarkably similar to Harrison's vision of the primordial, all-powerful mother goddess, who is later occluded by usurping male gods. In both cases, the feminine, the maternal, is older and gives rise to the masculine; the masculine then usurps and denies the feminine. But the masculine is only partially successful in its attempt to dominate and obscure the feminine. The feminine eventually reasserts herself over the course of time: the goddess over the course of Greek history and psychologically, the unconscious, feminine psyche's reassertion during the second half of life.

Neumann's view of the symbolic images produced by the psyche in the process of its maturation is strikingly similar to Harrison's outline of the evolution of the goddesses:

> In the early phase of consciousness, the numinosity of the archetype consequently exceeds man's power of representation, so much so that at first no form can be given to it. And when later the primordial archetype takes form in the imagination of man, its representations are often monstrous and

> inhuman. This is the phase of the chimerical creatures composed of different animals or of animals and man—the griffins, sphinxes, harpies, for example—and also of such monstrosities as phallic and bearded mothers. It is only when consciousness learns to look at phenomena from a certain distance, to react more subtly, to differentiate and distinguish, that the mixture of symbols prevailing in the primordial archetype separates into the groups of symbols characteristic of a single archetype or of a group of related archetypes: in short, that they became recognizable. (Neumann 2015: 12–13)

Like Bachofen, Harrison and Freud, Neumann accepted as factual the mythic narrative of primordial matriarchy; however, he saw its psychological analogue as far more important. This revisioning of the myth of the prehistorical goddess has allowed it to survive in the field of depth psychology even as it has lost its support among historians, archeologists, and classicists.

Walter Otto brought the Romantic project of resurrecting the gods and goddesses of classical antiquity nearly to completion. Otto saw the gods as manifestations of emotional and psychic states. Just as Homer saw the gods as acting upon humans, so Otto sees them as *happening* to us, as living *through* us and *in* us, whether we recognize them or not. Otto believed that the energies represented by the goddesses and gods are as alive today, in us, as they were when they were worshipped by the Greeks.

James Hillman, relying heavily upon the work of Otto, continued the project of recognizing the gods and goddesses as actual effective energies. For Hillman the number of divine beings is almost limitless since they are as numerous as the various emotional states we undergo. The gods constitute the psychic forces that live through us (Hillman 1976: 130). The myths of the gods correspond to the patterns by which our lives are constructed and through which we live. The myths are the structures that pattern our lives, they are the medium by which these divinities live through us.

Walter Burkert agreed with Harrison that the mystery cults evoked emotional experiences, but he differed from her in asserting that they were not associated with beliefs in or hopes for an afterlife. He goes to great lengths to disabuse us of the many modern misunderstandings of the mystery cults of antiquity. He asserts that they had no creeds or dogmas and provided no "salvation" from death. Burkert claims that they were not of late origin, not the result of foreign, Oriental influences, and, perhaps most surprisingly, that the mystery cults were not "mystical." Burkert acknowledged the reality of "things experienced" as well as of the "things done" in the mystery cults. Following Harrison, but without acknowledging her, Burkert defines the mysteries as "initiation rituals of a voluntary, personal, and secret character that aimed at a change of mind through experience of the sacred" (1987: 11). However, Burkert is very consistent in his assertion that the Mystery cults of the Greeks were not mystical, that they did not induce ecstatic, ineffable experiences: "If *mysticism* means personal introspection, the opening of a deeper dimension of the soul until a light shines forth within, then the Eleusinian Mysteries were precisely *un*-mystical" (1972: 248).

If Burkert was emphatic in his opinions on the "*un*-mystical" nature of the Eleusinian Mysteries, Harrison was less so. It is part of her genius that she raises more questions about the mystery religions than she answers. At the end of *Prolegomena* we too are left questioning. Characteristically, she leaves the issue open, reflecting perhaps her underlying ambivalence toward late Greek religion and to religion in general.

NOTES

1. Dionysos was considered by the Greeks to have come from Thrace. Later authors have sought his origin in Asia Minor, Crete, Egypt, or the Near East, but none of these has been conclusively confirmed. Walter Otto suggests that foreignness and "arrival" to his devotees is instead part of Dionysos's identity; that he was the god who arrived to his devotees, in the form of divine madness (Otto 1965: 79–85). Thus, his place of birth is of no real importance. The land where myth says he grew up, Nysa, is never given a precise location because such a location cannot be given: it is by definition a "foreign land." Dionysos is the embodiment of alterity,

the archetypal "Other." His foreignness is not due to his late arrival in Greece, but to the manner in which Dionysos manifests to humankind: arriving from "elsewhere" in ecstasy and divine madness.

2. Aspects of the Orpheus myth suggest that Orphism may have had an influence on the development of Christianity. Orpheus's descent to the Underworld to retrieve Eurydice mirrors Christ's descent to the Underworld (known in Christianity as "the Harrowing of Hell"). The bloody deaths of Orpheus and Dionysos by dismemberment prefigure the bloody death of Jesus Christ. Wine, which was a potent symbol for Orphism, became a sacrament for Christians.

   Asceticism characterizes both Orphism and Christianity (as it does Pythagoreanism as well). Finally, a blessed afterlife, unknown in Greece of the Archaic age and the Homeric epics, awaits initiates into the Orphic cult as it does for Christians.

3. Harrison anticipated Kerényi in her recognition of the possibility of the Egyptian origin of certain elements of Dionysian and Orphic cults. She cites Herodotus' account of Egyptian funeral customs: "In this they concur with the practices that are popularly known as Orphic and Bacchic, but are in fact Egyptian and Pythagorean" (Herodotus 2013: 140).

   Kerényi notes the remarkable similarity of the myth of Dionysos's death, dismemberment, and resurrection to the myths of Osiris. He proposed: Egyptian origins for certain elements of the cult of Dionysos, suggesting that Dionysos's association with beer (Kerényi 1976: 36), mead (1976: 37), and viticulture (1976: 56–57) all arrived in Greece from Egypt by way of Crete. He likewise proposed an Egyptian origin for Dionysos's associations with the ship, as in the myth of his abduction by ship and in the carrying of Dionysos's cult statue in a ship (1976: 165–67).

   Dionysos's wine festivals of Lenaia and Anthesteria were held in the late winter, after the cold weather had allowed the final clearing of the wine, making it drinkable. Despite the very different climates of Egypt and Greece, Kerényi points out that in Egypt, the night of January 5 since 1996 BC had been a festive date, marking the birth of light. On the island of Andros, after the introduction of the Julian calendar, the same date was set for a Dionysian miracle, the transformation of the water from a certain spring into wine—a form of the god's birth (1976: 299).

   The Greek festival of wine and the birth of the god coincides with the Egyptian festival of the birth of light.

4. The German Romantics' project of reinvigorating the polytheistic religion of ancient Greece is sometimes underappreciated. They delved deeply into the mythological and folkloric heritage of Greece, India, Egypt, Polynesia, and Germany because "myth is seen ... to have a religious quality; myth becomes a way of redeeming modern man and

restoring him to his early simplicity—his original and primeval union with God and nature" (Feldman and Richardson 1972: 297). Hölderlin "indeed, is an example of how far one could go in regarding ancient Greek myth as still-vital religion" (1972: 299). Hölderlin was among the first in this period of European history to recognize the reality of the Greek gods as such, a very radical proposal at the time.

5. Neumann (1905–1960), analytical psychologist and student of C. G. Jung, is best remembered for this theories on the emergence of consciousness. The best known among his many works are *The Origins and History of Consciousness* (1954) and *The Great Mother: An Analysis of the Archetype* (1955).

CONCLUSION

Jane Harrison is best known today as the founder of the group known today as the Cambridge Ritualists. However, her original ideas on Greek religion began long before this group came together and evolved greatly over time. The interests of the Cambridge Ritualists were quite various; they were never a monolithic group.

Harrison took up and advanced the argument in the myth and ritual school, regarding the primacy of one over the other. This argument remains unresolved today, and likely cannot be resolved, but it has generated a great deal of investigation and thought over the years. Harrison built on the anthropological work of William Robertson Smith and James George Frazer, but diverged significantly from them. While in *Prolegomena* Harrison adhered to the creed "myth is ritual misunderstood," by the time she wrote *Themis* and *Ancient Art and Ritual* she had modified this to an understanding that myth and ritual were complementary, that myth was the spoken counterpart to enacted ritual. Such flexibility of thought is admirable.

Harrison pioneered the interdisciplinary approach to classics that lies at the heart of classical studies today. In a field that had always been heavily text-centered, she brought in first the findings of archeology and recently discovered artworks, and later the findings of anthropology, sociology, and psychology. She was always drawn by her aesthetic sensibilities to the art of the Greeks, especially the sculptures and vase paintings of the archaic and early classical periods. This led her to see discrepancies between the textual accounts of myths and rituals and the ways they were depicted in art. This was the impetus for her first great work, *Prolegomena to the Study of Greek Religion*. This alone would have been enough to assure her a place in the history of the study of Greek religion. However, the working-out of her ideas did not stop there. After its publication her reading of Bergson, Durkheim, and Freud caused her to radically rethink her proposed origins of Greek religion. The result was *Themis* and *Ancient Art and Ritual*.

Harrison made the radically new proposal of the origin of Greek religion in *keres*, formless or partially embodied manifestations of emotion: fear, hunger, and desire. Harrison was one of the first to explore the prehistory of Greek religion, a study that continues actively today.

Harrison brought much needed attention to the importance of goddesses and women's rituals in Greek religion, arguing that goddesses arose before the gods and that for many centuries they were of far greater importance, and that women's rituals, in part because they were marginalized in antiquity, had retained elements of the earliest phases of Greek religion and thus provided material for study of that phase of religion. With these discoveries she opened up entirely new avenues of inquiry into women's cults and goddesses that have been explored ever since.

Harrison was not afraid of altering her thoughts regarding the origins of Greek religion. She was always generous to her colleagues, not only to those authors on whose work she built, but especially to her friends among the Cambridge Ritualists. She was, in my opinion, perhaps too generous. In *Themis*, she asked her friends, Cornford and Murray, to write two of the chapters: "The Origin of the Olympic Games" and "Excursus on the Ritual Forms preserved in Greek tragedy." These essays make for fascinating reading in their own way, but in her modesty in deferring to her male friends and colleagues she has deprived us of what I imagine could have been her unique insights on these rituals.

I admire Harrison's courage in her ability to surprise herself in discovering new ways of thinking, to the point even of contradicting her earlier writings. She trusted her feelings and intuitions, allowing them to influence her thinking and allowing her emotionally inflected thought to come through on the page. Her understanding of Greek religion, while always evidence-based, has a persuasive, emotional appeal.

At a time when academic thought was becoming increasingly hostile to religious feeling, Harrison went against this tendency when she discovered a deeply felt emotional and mystical sensibility in Greek religion—a feeling that she found to resound in herself. Early in her career she developed an aesthetic enthusiasm for Greek art. Later she became attentive to the emotional power of the *keres*, Dionysos, the women's cults and mystery cults, and above all to the goddesses. In view of her rejection of the religion of her childhood and her early, enthusiastic embrace of scientific methods, it may have come as a surprise to her when she discovered the power of the goddess, not only for the Greeks of antiquity but for herself.

Without ever abandoning the evidence-based approach, Harrison managed the difficult balancing of head and heart in her study of Greek religion. Many have since followed in her footsteps. We would be wise to honor one who first showed us the way.

REFERENCES

Ackerman, Robert. 1991a. *The Myth and Ritual School: J.G. Frazer and the Cambridge Ritualists*. New York: Routledge.

———. 1991b. "Introduction." In *Prolegomena to the Study of Greek Religion*, Jane Ellen Harrison. Princeton: Princeton University Press.

Aristotle. 2001. *The Basic Works of Aristotle*. ed. Richard McKeon. New York: Modern Library.

Bachofen, Johann Jakob. 1967. *Myth, Religion, and Mother Right: Selected Writings of JJ Bachofen*, trans. Ralph Manheim. Princeton: Princeton University Press.

Beard, Mary. 2000. *The Invention of Jane Harrison*. Cambridge: Harvard University Press.

———. 2010. "My hero: Jane Ellen Harrison." 2010. *The Guardian*, September 3. ISSN 0261-3077. Retrieved January 16, 2020 from https://www.theguardian.com/books/2010/sep/04/mary-ellen-harrison-mary-beard.

Bergson, Henri. [1911] 1998. *Creative Evolution*, trans. Arthur Mitchell. Mineola: Dover Publications.

Bošković, Aleksandar. 2021. *William Robertson Smith*. New York: Berghahn Books.

Burkert, Walter. 1983. *Homo Necans: The Anthropology of Ancient Greek Sacrificial Ritual and Myth*, trans. Peter Bing. Los Angeles: University of California Press.

———. 1985. *Greek Religion*, trans. John Raffan. Cambridge: Harvard University Press.

———. 1987. *Ancient Mystery Cults*. Cambridge: Harvard University Press.

Dodds, Eric. 1957. *The Greeks and the Irrational*. Boston: Beacon Press.

Downing, Christine. 2004. *The Luxury of Afterwards: The Christine Downing Lectures at San Diego State University 1995–2004*. New York: iUniverse.

———. 2018. *Mythopoetic Musings 2007–2018*. Echo Editions.

Ellenberger, Henri F. 1970. *The Discovery of the Unconscious: The History and Evolution of Dynamic Psychiatry*. New York: Basic Books.

Eller, Cynthia. 2000. *The Myth of Matriarchal Prehistory: Why an Invented Past Won't Give Women a Future*. Boston: Beacon Press.

Farnell, Lewis Richard. [1896] 2005. *The Cults of the Greek States, Vols. 1–5*. New York: Elibron Classics.

Frazer, James George. [1922] 1996. *The Golden Bough*. New York: Simon and Schuster.

Feldman, Burton and Robert D. Richardson, Jr. 1972. *The Rise of Modern Mythology: 1680–1860*. Indianapolis: Indiana University Press.

Freud, Sigmund. 1950. *Totem and Taboo: Some Points of Agreement between the Mental Lives of Savages and Neurotics*, trans. James Strachey. New York: W. W. Norton and Company.

———. 1961. *The Future of an Illusion*, trans. James Strachey. New York: W. W. Norton and Company.

———. 1965. *The Psychopathology of Everyday Life*, trans. James Strachey. New York: W. W. Norton and Company.

———. 1967. *Moses and Monotheism*, trans. Katherine Jones. New York: Vintage Books.

———. 1999. *The Interpretation of Dreams*, trans. Joyce Crick. Oxford: Oxford University Press.

———. 2013. *Civilization and its Discontents*. Seaside: Rough Draft Printing.

Gennep, Arnold van. [1909] 1960. *The Rites of Passage: A Classic Study of Cultural Celebrations*, trans. Monika Visedom and Gabrielle Caffee. Chicago: University of Chicago Press.

Gimbutas, Marija. 1974. *The Goddesses and Gods of Old Europe: Myths and Cult Images*. New York: Thames and Hudson.

Guthrie, W. K. C. 1955. *The Greeks and Their Gods*. Boston: Beacon Press.

Harrison, Jane Ellen. 1882. *Myths of the Odyssey in Art and Literature*. London: Rivingtons.

———. 1892. *Introductory Studies in Greek Art*. London: T. Fisher Unwin.

———. [1903] 1991. *Prolegomena to the Study of Greek Religion*. Princeton: Princeton University Press.

———. 1905. *The Religion of Ancient Greece*. Chicago: Open Court Publishing.

———. [1912] 1974. *Themis, A Study of the Social Origins of Greek Religion*.

———. [1913] 2007. *Ancient Art and Ritual*. New York: Forgotten Books.

———. [1915] 2018. *Alpha and Omega*. London: Sidgwick and Jackson.

———. 1921. *Epilegomena to the Study of Greek Religion*. New York: Cambridge University Press.

———. 1926. *Reminiscences of a Student's Life*. London: Hogarth Press.

Herodotus. 2013. *The Histories*, trans. Tom Holland. New York: Penguin Books.

Hillman, James. 1976. *Re-Visioning Psychology*. New York: Harper and Row.

Homer. 1998. *Iliad*, trans. Robert Fagles. New York: Penguin Books.

Hornblower, Simon and Antony Spawforth, eds. 2003. *The Oxford Classical Dictionary*. New York: Oxford University Press.

Jung, C. G. and Carl Kerényi. 1949. *Essays on a Science of Mythology: The Myth of the Divine Child and the Mysteries of Eleusis*. Bollingen Series XXII, trans. R. F. C. Hull. Princeton: Princeton University Press.

Kerényi, Carl. 1967. *Eleusis: Archetypal Image of Mother and Daughter*, trans. Ralph Manheim. Princeton: Princeton University Press.

———. 1976. *Dionysos: Archetypal Image of Indestructible Life*, trans. Ralph Manheim. Princeton: Princeton University Press.

Lopez-Pedraza, Rafael. 2000. *Dionysus in Exile: On the Repression of the Body and Emotion*. Wilmette: Chiron Publications.

McGinty, Park. 1978. *Interpretation and Dionysos: Method in the Study of a God*. New York: Mouton Publishers.

Müller, F. Max. 1869. "Comparative Mythology." In *Chips from a German Workshop, Vol. 2*. New York.

Neumann, Erich. 1994. *The Fear of the Feminine and Other Essays on Feminine Psychology*, trans. Boris Matthews, Esther Doughty, Eugene Rolfe, and Michael Cullingworth. Princeton: Princeton University Press.

———. 2015. *The Great Mother: An Analysis of the Archetype*, trans. Ralph Manheim. Princeton: Princeton University Press.

Nietzsche, Friedrich. 1993. *The Birth of Tragedy: Out of the Spirit of Music*, trans. Shaun Whiteside. New York: Penguin Books.

Nilsson, Martin Persson. [1940] 2007. *Greek Popular Religion*. Coppel: Forgotten Books.

Otto, Rudolph. 1923. *The Idea of the Holy: An Inquiry into the Non-Rational Factors in the Idea of the Divine and its Relation to the Rational*, trans. John W. Harvey. San Bernardino: Pantianos Classics.

Otto, Walter. 1954. *The Homeric Gods: The Spiritual Significance of Greek Religion*, trans. Moses Hadas. New York: Pantheon.

———. 1965. *Dionysus: Myth and Cult*. trans. Robert B. Palmer. Indianapolis: Indiana University Press.

Peacock, Sandra J. 1988. *Jane Ellen Harrison: The Mask and the Self*. New Haven: Yale University Press.

Robinson, Annabel. 2002. *The Life and Work of Jane Ellen Harrison*. New York: Oxford University Press.

Segal, Charles. 1986. *Interpreting Greek Tragedy: Myth, Poetry, Text*. Ithaca: Cornell University Press.

Segal, Robert A. 1980. "The Myth-Ritualist Theory of Religion." *Journal for the Scientific Study of Religion*: 173–85.

———. 1991. "Series Editor's Foreword." *The Myth and Ritual School*, Robert Ackerman. New York: Routledge.

———. ed. 1998a. *Jung on Mythology*. Princeton: Princeton University Press.

———. 1998b. *The Myth and Ritual Theory*. Malden: Blackwell Publishers.

———. 1999. *Theorizing About Myth*. Amherst: University of Massachusetts Press.

———. 2008. "William Robertson Smith vis-à-vis Émile Durkheim as Sociologist of Religion." *Journal of Scottish Thought*, 1–2: 1–12.

———. 2014. "Greek Myths and Psychoanalysis." In *Approaches to Greek Myth*, ed. Lowell Edmunds, 2nd edn. Baltimore: Johns Hopkins University Press.

———. 2015. *Myth: A Very Short Introduction*. Oxford: Oxford University Press.

Smith, William Robertson. [1889] 1894. *Lectures on the Religion of the Semites: First Series, The Fundamental Institutions. New Edition, revised throughout by the author*. London: Adam and Charles Black.

Snell, Bruno. [1953] 1982. *The Discovery of the Mind*, trans. T. G. Rosenmeyer. New York: Dover Publications.

Turner, Victor. [1969] 2008. *The Ritual Process: Structure and Anti-Structure*. New Brunswick: Aldine Transaction.

Verrall, Margaret DeG. 1890. *Mythology and Monuments of Ancient Athens: Being a Translation of a Portion of the Attica of Pausanias*. London: Macmillan and Company.

Wade, Francesca. 2020. *Square Haunting: Five Lives in London Between the Wars*. New York: Tim Duggan Books.

INDEX

Numbers in *italics* refer to illustrations.

www.ingramcontent.com/pod-product-compliance
Lightning Source LLC
La Vergne TN
LVHW012336130926
847902LV00028B/416
9781807580544